THE CHALLENGE OF ART TO PSYCHOLOGY

◆ THE CHALLENGE OF ART TO PSYCHOLOGY

SEYMOUR B. SARASON

YALE UNIVERSITY PRESS

NEW HAVEN ◆ LONDON

Russell Baker's "Getting Tired of High-Culture Humility" is copyright © 1988 by The New York Times Company. Reprinted by permission.

Excerpts from Kenneth Koch's *Wishes, Lies, and Dreams* and *I Never Told Anybody* are reprinted by kind permission of the author.

Set in New Baskerville type by The Composing Room of Michigan, Inc. Printed in the United States of America by Vail-Ballou Press, Binghamton, New York.

Library of Congress Cataloging-in-Publication Data
Sarason, Seymour Bernard, 1919–
    The challenge of art to psychology / Seymour B. Sarason.
        p.   cm.
    Includes bibliographical references.
    ISBN 0–300–04754–1
    1. Art—Psychology.   2. Creation (Literary, artistic, etc.)
3. Art and society.   I. Title.
N71.S18 1990
701'.15—dc20   89–21479
                                                              CIP

The paper in this book meets the guidelines for permanence and durability of the Committee on Production Guidelines for Book Longevity of the Council on Library Resources.

10 9 8 7 6 5 4 3 2 1

To Henry W. Schaefer-Simmern

December 11, 1896–October 16, 1978

CONTENTS

PREFACE

Choosing a title for a book can be a problem, especially if the substance of the book falls, so to speak, between the cracks of established disciplines or areas of inquiry. The one word in the title about which I had absolutely no qualms was *challenge*. What I had to say I intended as a challenge to existing psychologies—not to *a* psychology but to all psychologies that have some claim to intellectual legitimacy. Even so, the title I chose is probably not the most felicitous, if only because it does not convey the fact that these psychologies are suffused with overlearned meanings and cultural values that are distinctive features of our society.

My challenge goes beyond psychological theories. Indeed, I emphasize that what needs to be challenged are axioms which, if they continue to remain unexamined, will have a negative impact on our society's future. At stake is not art in any conventional sense but the ways in which people can experience satisfaction over their lifetimes from the ordered expression of their imagery, thoughts, and feelings. The satisfaction that comes from making something, and being made and formed by it, is missing in the lives of most people. Descartes said, "I think, therefore I am." Someone else said, "I scribble, therefore I am," a way of describing how artistic activity in its earliest manifestations is already a process of forming and being formed.

No developmental psychologist, theoretician, or researcher denies that artistic activity is a predictable function, observable in all young children in all cultures on this earth. Why, then, does this activity seem to get extinguished with the passing years? Why do most adults come to regard themselves as uncreative or unartistic? How do we explain the persistence of the view that artistic activity is a special feature of special people? These are some of the questions I take up in this book. The answers are only in part a consequence of the narrowness of extant psychologies. They require that we look at cultural attitudes, the socialization process, and educational practices, all of which combine to engender in people the feeling that artistic activity is alien to their capabilities. It is a classic case of the self-fulfilling prophecy and blaming the victim. The best title of the book from my standpoint would be: *How Our Society Ignores, Blunts, Extinguishes, and Devalues a Universal Feature of Human Capability, with Untoward Effects for People and the Society.* Too unwieldy—and besides, it does not contain the key words *art* or *artistic activity.*

The media through which artistic activity becomes manifest are many—music, dance, theater, radio, television, film, and others. If in this book I have concentrated on some of the visual arts and writing, it is not because I value them more highly than other media but rather because I know them better; and, as will become evident in later pages, I wished to emphasize the presence of the artistic process in activities we ordinarily ignore or misinterpret. This is by design not a scholarly book, if by that is meant a critical and comprehensive review of what others have said or studied. I am by no means the first person to assert that artistic activity is a universal feature of the human organism. Many people have made that assertion, but few have acted in ways consistent with it. What I have to say is based on the work of those few. That is why I have devoted so many pages to John Dewey, Henry Schaefer-Simmern, Kenneth Koch, and a handful of lesser-known people. As I will argue, the evidence for my assertion is scanty by the usual criteria of proof, but it certainly is compelling. It is also the case that I have had firsthand experience with a number of teachers who have demonstrated the validity of the assertion but whose accomplishments will never see the light of published day.

I am no optimist in regard to recent pronouncements and reports about an enlarged role for the arts in our schools. These are well-intentioned statements and proposals, but they will predictably fail of their purposes for precisely the same reasons that reforms of the science curriculum have been a total disaster. Why? Because the challenge concerns not only art or science education, but our conventional view of human nature and the ways that view suffuses the substance and organization of our schools. The nature of artistic activity and its universality have been inspiring to me because of their implications for what people can be and do at levels appropriate to their development and capability. However, this is no warrant for glossing over the fact that the gulf between what is and can be, what is and should be, seems unbridgeable. Between theory and practice, values and action, ideals and the social-cultural-institutional realities, lies a minefield of explosive obstacles. If I end this book on a somewhat pessimistic note, it is not because I am by temperament on the depressive side. It is simply because I feel that an upbeat ending would be unrealistic.

As usual, Dodie Allen, friend and secretary, was of invaluable help in preparing the manuscript for publication. I know when to thank God for big favors.

THE CHALLENGE OF ART TO PSYCHOLOGY

1 ◆ THE ARGUMENT

IN SUMMARY

This book is a challenge to conventional views of human nature. I do not mean platonic essences whose manifestations are inevitable. Rather, I mean the potential to develop mental processes and activities whose manifestations serve specific purposes. Those manifestations can and do vary dramatically within and among different cultures. Within any one culture they change over time. From the moment of birth human nature is social nature. Neonates, for example, obviously differ in terms of what we call temperament, but those differences have a different impact upon and elicit different responses from a social surround. The concepts of human nature and social nature are different linguistic expressions of an omnipresent transactional process.

By the phrase "potential to develop" I refer to activities (and their covert processes) that are observable in all human communities—for example, acquiring and using language, engaging in complicated sexual behavior, preparing and eating food, playing, fantasizing. Not all of these potentials are uniquely human, but the ways in which they are manifested in the human community are. Artistic activity is a unique, universal potential of the human organism, of all human organisms. I define artistic activity as an individual's choice and use of a particular medium to give ordered external expression to internal imagery, feelings, and ideas that are unique in some way for that individual. Copying is the polar opposite of artistic activity. Volumes have been written on the nature of creativity and the creative process. However much they differ in definition and emphasis, there is total agreement that the end product contains in some way the imprimatur of the maker.

That point has even been made in an arena that on the surface seems quite different from the artistic one. In the industrial literature, numerous writers have emphasized the many practical consequences of the differences between work and labor. Laboring is an activity whose products are completely unrelated to what the individual thinks, feels, imagines. The product of the assembly line remains the same independent of who is on the assembly line; the relation between product and "producer" is totally impersonal. Work, in contrast, is an activity that bears in some way and to some extent a personal signature. From this perspective, work and labor are not on the same continuum, just as copying and creating are not on the same continuum. Work and artistic activity *are* on the same continuum. Nothing has been more effective in obscuring the presence of artistic processes than the tendency to regard them as special features of special people, the most special of whom have their works exhibited in museums, galleries, or other sites. That the potential for artistic activity is universal is an assertion by no means new, but its implications and consequences have hardly been pursued. In what we colloquially call the real world, the gulf between assertion and practice is vast indeed.

Conceptions of what people are or could be have changed as worldviews have changed. Periclean Athens, the Renaissance, and the French Enlightenment are descriptive labels that convey very distinctive views about what people are, could be, and should be. Each major change in worldview is a reaction against and an exposé of the unverbalized axioms on which the previous worldview rested. Over time the new worldview falls captive to its particular axioms, as if finally eternal truths have been found that will not be supplanted by a new worldview. However great have been the changes in worldview in Western society, they have had little or no effect on the acceptance of the axiom that artistic activity is a special talent of special people. No one would contend that biologically intact humans can be divided into those who can run fast and those who cannot. Obviously some people can run faster than others, but we do not conclude from this fact that there are only two classes of humans. But that is precisely what we do conclude in regard to the potential for artistic activity and development.

It is that conclusion that this book calls into question. That similar challenges have been articulated with little or no consequence should occasion no surprise, because if the conclusion is invalid in whole or in part, it requires that we reexamine the nature and purposes of our society, the ways in which we customarily regard ourselves and others. One worldview does not surrender peacefully to another. Changes in worldviews are always seen in retrospect as cataclysmic in their consequences over time—cataclysmic for the supplanted worldview.

In whatever ways we label or demarcate an era and characterize its dominant worldview, certain events stand out as a kind of watershed. They give increased force and clarity to the worldview at the same time that they stimulate alterations in it. World War II is one of those watersheds in the modern era because it catapulted issues about human potential onto the world scene in a most dramatic way. German nazism, Italian fascism, Japanese imperialism, and Stalinist tyranny (each of which was responsible for the deaths of millions before the war, although the dimensions of the cruelties became clearer afterwards) forced people to reconsider the human potential for destructive aggression. It was hard to continue to hold a benign view of human nature. The Nazi effort to destroy European Jewry, the Japanese atrocities in China, and Stalin's murder of millions of Russian citizens were potent antidotes to the belief in man's goodness. There are many today who, when they read about these events, find them hard to credit and seek explanations that enable them to hold onto the belief that these happenings are but jogs in a steadily onward and upward climb to a humane civilization.

In contrast, the political consequences of World War II, within and among old and new nations, gave a new dynamism to such concepts as freedom, human rights, equality, and individuals' claims to opportunities for growth and expression. A change occurred in how the nature of human nature was regarded. What heretofore had been honored largely (although not exclusively) on the level of rhetoric now began to be taken more seriously in practice. In our own society, diverse groups, notably women, blacks, and other minorities, essentially began to redefine themselves in terms of capabilities and status, explicitly challenging culturally regnant conceptions of human potential.

Elsewhere (Sarason, 1977) I have discussed the sea-swell significances of these changes, labeling the post–World War II era as one in which "redefinition of self as resource" occurred. Phrases like "human potential," "self-realization," "lifelong learning," "personal fulfillment," and "personal authenticity" entered the language. It is not an exaggeration to say that meeting the demands for personal growth and expression became an industry. Do women have the potential to become first-rate scientists or mathematicians? Do blacks have the same pattern of cognitive abilities as whites? Are people doomed to experience a decline in mental functioning with age? Whatever else such questions signify, they demonstrate how issues about human potential have taken on new force and status on the public agendas. If the war brought recognition that man's capacity for inhumanity is not minuscule (although memories and knowledge of the conflict fade with the passing of years), issues surrounding the nature of human abilities, far from fading, seem to engender more controversy in the world of theory and practical affairs.

Although this book is a challenge to conventional ways of conceptualizing human potential, it is not part of any ongoing controversy. It is considered self-evident that artistic activity is a special ability of special people. No psychological theory of human development to my knowledge even suggests that the capacity for artistic development is uniquely human and that its flowering or extinction is crucial for understanding a culture. Art as process and product has no special significance for psychological theories. In the search for universal features and laws of human behavior and development, art has escaped notice by theorists—except, as I indicate in later chapters, for John Dewey, who stands alone in this regard. Alone and unread, at least in psychology.

I regard the contents of this book as an elaboration of Dewey's views as expressed in his book *Art as Experience* (1934). My own argument can be summarized as follows:

1. The capacity for artistic expression and development is universal. If there is agreement about anything in the research and observational literature on artistic activity, it is that such activity appears to be universal in young children. The literature also suggests that artistic activity in our culture, in terms of interest and engagement, seems to vanish over the years of schooling, except in a tiny number of individuals.

2. To the earliest manifestations of artistic activity, the prepotent response is one that considers how well the product squares with "reality"—that is, how representational or recognizable the contents or forms are. Little or no attention, let alone praise, is given to how the individual uses a medium (for example, line and color in a visual product) in an ordered way that reflects his or her internal imagery or conception. The affective response of liking or disliking a product and the dominance of the criterion of representing reality effectively prevent recognition of the degree to which the product is an integrated whole—that is, its gestalt-like qualities.

3. Ours is not a culture that places a premium on the artistic activity of young children. Scores of child-rearing books sensitize parents to the importance of reading, writing, numbers, and "objective" thinking as necessary for the good life. They say nothing about artistic activity as a source of personal expression, mastery, and satisfaction over a lifetime.

4. Artistic activity is extinguished relatively early in life in large part

because of the individual's feeling of inadequacy in representing reality, the belief that artistry is a talent or gift that few possess, and intimidation by the perceived gulf between what the individual can do and what great artists have done. The result is a form of learned helplessness or inadequacy.

5. How do we explain the presence *and development* of artistic activity in visual or verbal media in individuals who heretofore have never been creative or in whom such activity would not have been predicted? I will refer specifically to the work of Henry Schaefer-Simmern and Kenneth Koch. The former worked with institutionalized, mentally retarded individuals as well as "ordinary" people, and the latter with black and Hispanic elementary schoolchildren in a ghetto school as well as with aged, ill, relatively uneducated residents in a conventional (= depressing) nursing home on New York's Lower East Side.

6. The need, indeed yearning, for artistic expression is never truly extinguished. It goes underground, a festering source of dissatisfaction in quotidian living. In recent decades, as longevity has increased as well as the percentage of the population who are aged, many of these individuals begin to engage—in their own way and at their own level—in an artistic activity for which they had considered themselves inadequate or unfavored by fate or opportunity.

7. It is unnecessary for my argument to discuss or speculate about genetic factors that may contribute to individual differences in artistic expression, its timing, pace, quality, and level. Whatever such factors are or turn out to be, they are not or will not be in conflict with the basic hypothesis that all people have the capacity to engage in and derive satisfaction from artistic activity in some way at some level.

8. What is at issue is not artistic activity per se but rather how worldviews, which are always about the nature of human nature, inevitably constrain our thinking about what people are and could be.

If I have kept my argument within narrow bounds, its implications are the opposite of narrow, if only because it requires that we view a particular human capability from an unaccustomed perspective. I assume that most readers, like myself, will find themselves asking the question: "If I take the argument seriously, what does it mean for, among other things, child rearing, education, leisure, and societal values?" For myself, I have concluded that *at this time* the question may well be a distraction because it can short-circuit the importance of examining the argument in terms of one's own life and one's observations of the lives of other people. The argument is not an exercise in logic, conceptualization, or theory. It is an outgrowth of personal turmoil and experience, mine and those of others, a dissatisfaction with the myriad ways in which we are effectively socialized to regard ourselves as nonartists.

Although I shall, for illustrative purposes, refer largely to visual art and writing, it should go without saying that artistic activity is manifested in diverse media. Many of these are not customarily associated with such activity and are engaged in by people who are not regarded as artists and who have been schooled to regard themselves as nonartists. That is one of my major themes: how a narrow conception of artistic activity prevents us from recognizing the presence of the artistic process. Although I touch upon the aesthetic response to works of art, that response is not central to my argument, which focuses on the artistic process as a way of ordering self and media, an ordering that is developmentally intrinsic to the need for mastery and personal expression. The emphasis is on the configuring properties of the process, independent of whether the artistic product is simple or complex and of our affective response to it. Truly to recognize and respect the artistic process requires that we go beyond expressions of liking and disliking, approving and disapproving. A wrong answer to an item in an intelligence test is a wrong *answer;* it does not warrant the conclusion that the individual did not employ, or is incapable of employing, the process used by someone who gave the right answer. Similarly, we may not like what an artist has done, but that is no warrant for glossing over the problem with which the artist struggled and the means he or she employed. Another artist faced with the same problem may come up with something more to our liking, but that does not justify us in ignoring what the two artists have in common in terms of process.

Nothing contributes more to a superficial aesthetic response than the overlearned belief of most people that they are incapable of engaging in artistic activity or have never engaged in such activity. That is to say, there is nothing in their experience that permits them to identify with the artistic process involved in giving ordered expression externally to an internal idea, a conception, a picture. Taught to regard themselves as artistic ciphers, they have no basis for appreciation or respect when confronted with a work of art. They stay on the level of liking or disliking. To regard them as philistines is a classic case of blaming the victim. Works of art can and should be judged from numerous perspectives. The perspective adopted in this book allows me to view artistic activity in terms of, first, of its universality and, second, of how our culture effectively ignores and subverts the development of that activity, with negative consequences for how lives are lived.

Given the thrust of this book, it will surprise no one that I look at our educational institutions, not with the intent of scapegoating their inadequacies of rationale and practice, but because what they do in regard to education in the arts so clearly reflects society's worldview. If our schools have the narrowest conception of human potential and the centrality of the representational process in giving ordered expression to experience, it is because they do not comprehend what Elliott Eisner said in his book *Cognition and Curriculum* (1982), an elaboration of his 1979 John Dewey lecture:

Insofar as education is concerned with developing the individual's ability to secure diverse forms of meaning through experience, then the ability to encode and decode the content embodied in different forms of representation is also of crucial importance. Such ability can be regarded as a form of literacy. The concept of literacy, as I have used it, is not limited to things said; it extends to things represented. I choose to use the term generically as the power to encode or decode meaning through any of the forms that humans use to represent what they have come to know. (P. xii)

It is not by happenstance, given Eisner's position, that he says:

Speaking of the physical costs of unfulfilled potential, the American poet John Ciardi, addressing a group of powerful, practical-minded businessmen, had this to say: 'There is no poetry for the practical man. There is poetry for the mankind of the man who spends a certain amount of his life turning the mechanical wheel. For if he spends too much of his time at the mechanics of practicality he must become something less than a man or be eaten up by the frustrations stored in his irrational personality.

'An ulcer, gentlemen, is an unkissed imagination taking its revenge for having been jilted. It is an unwritten poem, an undanced dance, an unpainted watercolor. It is a declaration from the mankind of the man that a clear spring of joy has not been tapped and that it must break through muddily, on its own'." (Eisner, 1982, p. 80)

Although I plead in this book for going beyond expressions of liking and disliking works of art, I do not mean to downplay their significances, especially in regard to their culturally loaded origins. Disliking a work of art frequently has a significance beyond what it says about an individual responder. That is to say, the affective response may be so widespread that, despite the recognition of the work as serious and important, the work engenders dislike or disinterest, raising an intriguing question about the relationship between artistic form and aesthetic response. For example, in an article "Atonal Music and Its Limits," Ribe (1987) discusses Schoenberg's creation of atonality early in this century.

The importance of Schoenberg's achievement is hard to exaggerate. The contemporary composer and theorist George Perle, for example, claims that the development of atonality by Schoenberg and his students "probably represents the most far-reaching and thoroughgoing revolution the history of music has known since the beginnings of polyphony." Schoenberg himself clearly recognized the significance of his method, of which he said: "I have made a discovery that will assure the supremacy of German music for the next hundred years."

Yet while composers of all nationalities have been influenced by Schoenberg's method, and the basic principles of atonal composition he introduced are still being employed today, the method has met with hardly any appreciation or acceptance from the public at large. Concert audiences continue to prefer the music of the past, and seem uninterested in even a limited exposure to atonal music. As a consequence, only a handful of atonal works are performed by our major musical organizations, which rely largely on the repertoire of earlier centuries to keep their audiences satisfied. Active appreciation of atonal music has thus been confined to a relatively few conductors and performers—and, of course, its composers.

Ribe concludes his thoughtful essay with these words:

> If tonality is natural, are some tonalities more natural than others? The question is dangerous, because no musical system is natural without qualification. Each was developed by a particular people at a particular time, and for a different purpose. In short, all musical systems are conventional. Nature provides the elements that make musical expression possible; convention shapes these elements into expressive musical works. . . .
>
> Western tonality owes its greatness to a set of conventions which allowed an unprecedented synthesis of expressive richness and formal control, of what Nietzsche called "enthusiasm" and "self-possession." The tragedy of Schoenberg's attempt to reestablish this synthesis was that the conventions he chose violated the constraints which nature had provided.
>
> It remains to be seen whether the future of Western music can equal the achievements of its past. The essence of the musical art, however, will remain what it has always been: to discover those conventions which most fully realize the natural expressive possibilities of tone.

The affective response, however superficial, can be revealing of what Ribe calls the limits of the artistic form, however innovative and complicated.

When I use the terms *artistic activity* or *artistic process*—or what we are duty-bound to seek to appreciate in their end products—I refer to the ways in which "materials" are used and configured to give us what an individual struggled to represent for him- or herself as well as for others. The pianist and critic Samuel Lipman (1987) has said it well: "What Bach teaches us is the primacy of the musical material, the value of each note and each combination of notes, of each melodic line and each combination of melodic lines. The beauty of Bach inheres as much in the parts as in the whole. Every separate line possesses its own interest, vitality, and autonomy; every moment is capable of standing alone before music's and Bach's God. Thus what we learn from Bach is that every note, every player, every musical thought counts."

What Lipman says about great artists is no less true for any work of art, however uncomplicated it may be, comparatively speaking. Artistic activity is the opposite of random activity. It is a process in which self and materials are configured. That you may not "like" the end product is no warrant for ignoring its gestalt-like character. More to the point of this book, ignoring that character contributes mightily to our misreading of the developmental significances of artistic activity in people generally.

A more general and historically based statement of what Lipman says about music is contained in Kahler's *Disintegration of Form in the Arts* (1968). I did not know Kahler, but from his writings I have to conclude that the conceptual kinship between him and Schaefer-Simmern (whose ideas and works inform later chapters of this book) is more than matched by their passionate concern, indeed anxiety, about the increasing correlation between societal and technological transformations on the one hand, and the disintegration of form in the arts on the other hand. Kahler concludes his discussion of "the forms of form" by saying:

> I have dealt so elaborately with the meaning and the problems of form because I believe them to be crucial not only in regard to art, but in regard to our whole human condition. We live in an era of transition, in which age-old modes of existence, and with them old concepts and structures, are breaking up, while new ones are not as yet clearly recognizable. In such a state of flux— more rapidly moving than ever—in the incessant turmoil of novelty of discoveries, inventions and experiments, in such a state, concepts like wholeness, like coherence, like history are widely discredited and looked upon with distrust and dislike. Not only are they felt to be encumbering the freedom of new ventures, they are considered obsolete and invalid. The repudiation of all these concepts implies a discarding of form, for they all—wholeness, coherence, history—are inherent in the concept of form. They all mean and constitute *identity*. Indeed, form may be plainly understood as identity. As Richard Blackmur strikingly put it: "Form is the limiting principle by which a thing is itself." Accordingly, losing form is equivalent to losing identity. (P. 21)

2 ◆ WORLDVIEW, INTELLIGENCE, AND PSYCHOLOGICAL TESTS

In any society of which we have a record, its people have a sense of a past that in some important ways distinguishes it from the present. In nonliterate societies that sense of a difference is contained in legend and myth. In the last several centuries the intrusion by Western peoples into such societies has given that sense of difference, of change, an all too poignant basis in personal experience. Western libraries are crammed with books describing and judging how the present differs from the past. One of the fascinating consequences of the study of the past is the flushing out and illuminating how, in what we call "eras," people had a conception of the nature of man that differed discernibly from that of the authors' time. So it becomes obvious that the conception of the nature of man in the Middle Ages differs significantly from that in the Renaissance, or the Reformation, or the era of the American and French revolutions—or, of course, today. If we feel an affinity with Periclean Athens, we know it is an affinity and not an identity.

Interest in and controversy about the nature of man have been distinguishing features of Western societies in the past several centuries. This interest has been both a cause of and a response to social, political, and religious changes and upheavals that made the nature of man a passionate concern. Where you stood about that concern made a difference in the quotidian world; it was no arid or abstract exercise. If Rousseau's writings received wide recognition in Western Europe, it was because his conception of the nature of man represented a critique of society and how it distorted and suffocated individuals' intellectual and social capabilities. Not everyone was receptive to Rousseau's ideas, but no one could deny the practical significance of explaining and justifying what man is, could be, should be.

In our own century Freud has played a similar role. Freud was far less explicit than Rousseau about societal structure, context, and dynamics, but it was clear that he was presenting a conception of the nature of man that had broad, if ambiguous, implications for what society should be. Both Rousseau and Freud posed the issue as the individual *versus* society. Karl Marx was far less of a psychologist, but even so his social-historical view and political activism rest on a conception of what man is, could be, should be—and, of course, he too saw society as inimical to the manifestation of human potential. Marx's conception of the nature of man has been criticized as utopian in the extreme. That criticism is valid, but it does not explain why millions of people embraced his notion of human potential, and it deflects attention from the fact that how one regards that potential is fateful in the world of social action.

Until the nineteenth century those who wrote about the nature and limits of human potential were not specialists; they were, broadly speaking, social philosophers acutely sensitive to a world that was changing and in conflict. In the second half of the nineteenth century, thinking and writing about human potential started to become the province of those who studied it within the emerging traditions of empirical science. It was at this time that psychology as a discipline began to emerge, to dissociate itself from philosophy, and to seek to establish itself as a scientific enterprise. This was, of course, the time that science as a way of understanding and influencing the social and physical world came into its own, the wave of a future of limitless possibilities. For example, until the latter half of the nineteenth century, "scientific medicine" hardly existed. What then passed for medical schools were largely commercial institutions, unaffiliated with hospitals or universities. Indeed, it was the deplorable (if not scandalous) state of medical education and its nonscientific underpinnings that stimulated the pathbreaking study in 1910 *Medical Education in the United States and Canada* by Abraham Flexner. You cannot read that report and not sense the passion with which Flexner emphasized his conclusions: medicine had to be grounded in the basic sciences, and the university was the prime setting for the wedding of science and medicine. Flexner's report did not produce a revolution; it was a catalyst for a focus contained in a zeitgeist at the center of which was a vision of a scientific future.

One of the consequences of Flexner's report was the age of specialization, leading to the phenomenon of specialties within specialties. This had already begun to happen at the end of the nineteenth century, when psychology started to become an independent discipline in the university. Psychologists set their sights on a future when psychology—the study of the mind—would unravel and illuminate human behavior and potential. This would be accomplished by following the traditions, values, and methodologies of science: clear statements of theory, rigorously designed and quantitatively analyzed studies (preferably experimental in nature), findings that were replicable, all suffused with a passion for objectivity. If only because the early psychologists sought to divorce their subject from philosophy, the "big" questions philosophy asked about human behavior and potential were replaced by smaller ones. It was as if an emphasis on methodology and quantification required that the mind be viewed as a strange clock whose parts needed to be identified and their mechanisms understood. Memory, reaction time, sensory discrimination, concept formation, mental set, imagery, judgment—these and other elements of mind and behavior became foci of study, each giving rise to a competing theory, as "laboratories" produced an increasing stream of published studies. Because it soon became apparent that for certain problems, using humans in the laboratory did not permit the isolation and experimental manipulation of mechanisms of learning and acquisition, as well as strength of motivation, a significant number of psychologists began to use rats, cats, and dogs. Just as the physicist sought the basic laws of matter in the mysteries of the atom, the psychologist sought to take apart the human mind, to establish the laws governing its workings.

Psychology did not need the equivalent of a Flexner report to justify its quest to become a scientific enterprise. The founders of psychology knew science: its history, accomplishments, ever-increasing status, and promise. And they were no less knowledgeable about the parent field of philosophy. It was not that they rejected the substantive concerns of philosophy—for example, the nature of the human mind and how it ordered and comprehended the world. Rather, they disdained its baggage of assumptions and concepts that were either unnecessary or untestable or too embedded in traditional theology. To my knowledge, none of these early psychologists wrote off philosophy as unimportant and fruitless for understanding man's place in the world. They were respectful of questions about values and ultimate purpose. Their stance was positive, not negative: these larger questions could be clarified only by the scientific study of mind and behavior leading to the establishment of laws on the basis of which actions relevant to the larger questions could be taken.

This stance was based on the unverbalized assumption that questions about human values and purpose—their origins, vicissitudes, and consequences—could be ignored or set aside as one sought the laws of mind and behavior. Put another way, the workings of the human mind could be understood independent of the time, place, and era of the mind and behavior of those being studied and those doing the studying. The possibility that this assumption might be invalid, even in part, was simply never raised. It could not have been raised at that time. As a consequence, psychology became the study of individuals apart from their era and society, and their place in them. Psychology came to have a social focus only in the sense that some psychologists (social psychologists) fastened on interpersonal—that is, dyadic—relationships. But it was and is not social in the broad social-cultural-class sense, a point beautifully made by John Dollard in his scandalously unheeded *Criteria for the Life History* (1935).

The emergence of modern psychology in the university was fateful in that it placed the psychologist in a setting that was, phenomenologically speaking, walled off from the larger society. Imagery of the laboratory—encapsulated physically, replete with instrumentation, restricted in substantive focus, producing data capable of quantitative analysis—was dominant and widespread. Problems that did not lend themselves to research in the laboratory tended not to be studied. It was not, it should be emphasized, that those early psychologists were unaware of the larger issues—such as the nature and course of human potential—but rather that they believed clarification would come only after the scientific analysis of the components of mind. The whole would be constructed from the parts, some day. Anyone who needs convincing on this score should read Hilgard's (1978) collection of presidential addresses to the American Psychological Association.

There were some notable exceptions like William James, who looked askance at psychology's tendency to focus primarily on problems amenable to laboratory study. Indeed, his wide-ranging interests, the kinds of issues he raised, made it all too easy for psychology to regard him primarily as a philosopher, not as a scientific psychologist. He "once" was a psychologist and then "became" a philosopher. It is hard to escape the conclusion that he was pigeonholed as a philosopher less because of the issues he raised than because he had eschewed the methodologies of the laboratory. That did not bother James, who regarded philosophy as the home of the larger issues about man in the world.

The most stirring exception was John Dewey. In his earliest papers, at the end of the nineteenth century, Dewey was already criticizing explanations of human behavior and potential that were not genetic or developmental in direction and that arbitrarily separated mind from culture and social context. In 1902, in the May issue of the *Psychological Review,* he published a paper entitled "Interpretation of the Savage Mind." Because that paper is not readily accessible, and because the initial pages are so distinctively Deweyan, prodromal of so much in his later writings, I reproduce here those opening pages:

> The psychical attitudes and traits of the savage are more than stages through which mind has passed, leaving them behind. They are outgrowths which have entered decisively into further evolution, and as such form an integral part of the framework of present mental organization. Such positive significance is commonly attributed, in theory at least, to animal mind; but the mental structure of the savage, which presumably has an ever greater relevancy for genetic psychology, is strangely neglected.
>
> The cause of this neglect I believe lies in the scant results so far secured, because of the abuse of the comparative method—which abuse in turn is due to the lack of a proper method of interpretation. Comparison as currently employed is defective—even perverse—in at least three respects. In the first place, it is used indiscriminately and arbitrarily. Facts are torn loose from their context in social and natural environment and heaped miscellaneously together, because they have impressed the observer as alike in some respect. Upon a single page of Spencer which I chanced to open in looking for an illustration of this point, appear Kamschadles, Kirghiz, Bedouins, East Africans, Bechuanas, Damaras, Hottentots, Malays, Papuans, Fijians, Andamanese—all cited in reference to establishing a certain common property of primitive minds. What would we think of a biologist who appealed successively to some external characteristic of, say, snake, butterfly, elephant, oyster and robin in support of a statement? And yet the peoples mentioned present widely remote cultural resources, varied environments and distinctive institutions. What is the scientific value of a proposition thus arrived at?
>
> In the second place, this haphazard, uncontrollable selection yields only static facts—facts which lack the dynamic quality necessary to a genetic consideration. The following is a summary of Mr. Spencer's characterizations of primitive man, emotional and intellectual:
>
> He is explosive and chaotic in feeling, improvident, childishly mirthful, intolerant of restraint, with but small flow of altruistic feeling, attentive to meaningless detail and incapable of selecting the facts from which conclusions may be drawn, with feeble grasp of thought, incapable of rational surprise, incurious, lacking in ingenuity and constructive imagination. Even the one quality which is stated positively, namely, keenness of perception, is interpreted in a purely negative way, as a character antagonistic to reflective development. 'In proportion as the mental energies go out in restless per-

ception, they cannot go out in deliberate thought.' And this from a sensationalist in psychology!

Such descriptions as these also bear out my first point. Mr. Spencer himself admits frequent and marked discrepancies, and it would not be difficult to bring together a considerable mass of proof-texts to support the exact opposite of each of his assertions. But my point here is that present civilized mind is virtually taken as a standard, and savage mind is measured off on this fixed scale.

It is no wonder that the outcome is negative; that primitive mind is described in terms of "lack," "absence": its traits are incapacities. Qualities defined in such fashion are surely useless in suggesting, to say nothing of determining, progress, and are correspondingly infertile for genetic psychology, which is interested in becoming, growth, development.

The third remark is that the results thus reached, even passing them as correct, yield only loose aggregates of unrelated traits—not a coherent scheme of mind. We do not escape from an inorganic conglomerate conception of mind by just abusing the "faculty" psychology. Our standpoint must be more positive. We must recognize that mind has a pattern, a scheme of arrangement in its constituent elements, and that it is the business of a serious comparative psychology to exhibit these patterns, forms or types in detail. By such terms, I do not mean anything metaphysical; I mean to indicate the necessity of a conception such as is a commonplace with the zoologist. Terms like articulate or vertebrate, carnivore or herbivore, are "pattern" terms of the sort intended. They imply that an animal is something more than a random composite of isolated parts, made by taking an eye here, an ear there, a set of teeth somewhere else. They signify that the constituent elements are arranged in a certain way; that in being co-adapted to the dominant functions of the organism they are of necessity co-related with one another. Genetic psychology of mind will advance only as it discovers and specifies generic forms or patterns of this sort in psychic morphology.

It is a method for the determination of such types that I wish to suggest in this paper. The biological point of view commits us to the conviction that mind, whatever else it may be, is at least an organ of service for the control of environment in relation to the ends of the life process.

It is not happenstance that this paper was written six years after Dewey had started a school for children at the University of Chicago and three years after his presidential address entitled "Psychology as Social Practice" to the American Psychological Association. In his writings and his creation of the school, Dewey's thinking was influenced by one assumption and one observation. The assumption was that human potential and its expressions, *or its lack of expressions,* were not comprehensible apart from the organism's transactions with its social-cultural surround. The observation was that our schools were discouragingly efficient in masking or inhibiting expressions of human potential. The schools reflected the larger social order. As Dewey said in his presidential address:

> The existing order is determined, neither by fate nor by chance, but is based on law and order, on a system of existing stimuli and modes of reaction, through knowledge of which we can modify the practical outcome. There is no logical alternative save either to recognize and search for the mechanism of the interplay of personalities that controls the existing distribution of values, or to accept as final a fixed hierarchy of persons in which the leaders assert, on no basis save their own supposed superior personality, certain ends and laws which the mass of men passively receive and imitate. The effort to apply psychology to social affairs means that the determination of ethical values lies not in any set or class, however superior, but in the workings of the social whole; that the explanation is found in the complex interactions and interrelations which constitute this whole. (*The Psychological Review* 1900: 105–24)

If Dewey left open the nature and limits of human potential, he was clear that the ultimate answer could not be independent of the existing social order, the ways in which the past of that order had been transformed into a present that was moving to a future. For Dewey the human animal was intelligent, but intelligence was not a faculty of the mind— that is, an element or factor, or a part among parts, or a platonic essence. Nor was intelligence a quantity of "something" of which some people had more and others less. Humans, at least biologically intact ones, were intelligent in that they were question-asking, question-answering, questing, purposeful, impactful, proactive organisms, constructing and reordering themselves and their worlds. Some have argued that Dewey had an unrealistically optimistic view of the nature and scope of human potential or intelligence, and that his social activism was no less visionary. I shall return to this argument in a later chapter, where I discuss what I regard as one of the twentieth century's classics: Dewey's *Art as Experience*. Suffice it to say here that Dewey destroys the dichotomy, sanctioned by custom, of art and non-art, the artist and the non-artist. For Dewey, artistic activity was a human attribute expressed or suppressed in myriad ways depending on features of the social context and the wider culture.

The third exception from those early days was the French psychologist Alfred Binet. Most people, including psychologists, associate his name only with the intelligence scales he developed. The historical absurdity symbolized by that association is well described in Theta

Wolf's biography (1973). The fact is that by temperament, conceptual concerns, and social outlook, Binet was kin to Dewey, though more like a cousin than a brother. Binet never deluded himself into thinking that his scales captured the complexities of human intelligence or that one could explain test performance independent of social-cultural contexts (or "national character") or that performance was other than a frail reed on which to rest conclusions about potential. To Binet, who coined the phrase "mental orthopedics," performance was but a goad to altering and improving performance. Intelligence was not a once-and-for-all thing; *it could be developed.* Test performance was the first step in a process that led to interventions in the classroom for the purpose of altering teacher-child transactions. Binet, like Dewey, was quintessentially experimental: before you accept an explanation of performance, he argued, try systematically to alter it.

There is no doubt that Dewey's conception of human intelligence derived from, among other things, the fact that he was a rural Vermonter troubled by the consequences of the industrialization of America. That he was a fervent supporter of Jane Addams's settlement house in Chicago should occasion no surprise. He was an astute observer of and responder to the societal scene. That was no less true of Binet, who was well aware of the problems, inadequacies, and inequities of the French schools struggling with the consequences of compulsory education. The conventional story is that the Parisian authorities asked Binet to devise a more valid means of assessing the potentials of schoolchildren, especially those who appeared to be mentally retarded. Wolf documents that the social activist Binet maneuvered to get the authorities to ask him to take on the task. His position was that issues around the nature and limits of human intelligence did not arise in a social vacuum but were *public* issues demanding the formulation and implementation of public policies. And precisely because these were public issues demanding action, it was not surprising that officialdom, the dominant social classes, proclaimed views that would be least upsetting to the existing social order. Central to those views was the belief that intelligence was a "thing," a kind of global capacity, which some people had more of than others because of heredity and/or embeddedness in a *sub*cultural context—deviation from the prevailing conception of how life should be lived. Dewey and Binet ran against the tide, not only the public tide but that of their discipline as well.

Nowhere more than in America did the nature of intelligence and its development become a public issue. That was guaranteed by the waves of immigration beginning in the middle of the nineteenth century and continuing until World War I. All of these immigrant groups were viewed as potential threats to the stability of the culture and the social order. They teemed into the cities with their strange tongues, dress, and "minds." Delinquency, crime, prostitution, feeblemindedness, and family disorganization escalated in frequency. And few things were as powerfully explanatory to the "native" stock as the low intelligence of these immigrant groups. Genetics as etiology and eugenics as practice began to inform public policy and action. This in large measure explains why some American psychologists (Goddard, Terman, Kuhlmann) made it their business to read or visit Binet to learn about the scales he had developed. If indeed he had come up with a way of "measuring" intelligence, it would have enormous practical value for locating and segregating the intellectually unfit and the intellectually gifted. Its applicability to the screening of immigrants seeking entry to this country was obvious.

What happened, as Wolf points out, is that the American psychologists took over Binet's methodology and ignored his questions and doubts about the adequacy of his scales in regard to the nature and expressions of human potential. They did more than take over his methodology; they sought to improve it by refinements in sampling, quantification, objectivity—all the trappings of what they saw as scientifically required and justified. It was the triumph of the technological over the theoretical, the philosophical, the speculative. Controversy soon arose about the composition of intelligence. Was it a general attribute, or was it comprised of separate abilities or factors, such as memory, concept formation, and so on? As statistical theory became more sophisticated, giving rise to new ways of analyzing test scores, controversy about methodology grew apace.

The emergence of intelligence tests gave expression to conventional conceptions of human potential and its vicissitudes. These conceptions rested on several assumptions. The first was in two parts, one obvious and one less so. The obvious part was that, however defined, intelligence was a normally distributed human attribute. The less obvious part was that intelligence changed little over the course of a lifetime; the proof rested on a cascade of studies demonstrating that test scores predicted school performance very well. It went relatively unnoticed that intelligence tests were constructed so as to make such predictions possible and valid. School performance was the major criterion for validation; that is, the "abilities" required for school performance were the abilities the tests had to measure. The possibility that schooling—its foci, goals, pedagogy, and culture—masked, suppressed, or ignored some universal human cognitive attributes and abilities was not raised. It was as if schooling required, stimulated, and nurtured all of the most distinctive aspects of human potential. If that was not the case, as it was not and is not, conceptions of intelligence and human potential were at best narrow, and at worst perpetrators of socially acceptable myth.

The second (and related) assumption was that problem-solving ability and behavior within and outside the testing situation were highly correlated. Relevant here is a series of experiences that led me to question that assumption. My first position as a psychologist was in a new state institution for the mentally retarded in the middle of nowhere in rural Connecticut. On my first day there I was part of a posse searching for a resident who had run away. Within that first year more than a score of runaways were recorded. Before those events I had given psychological tests to almost all of them. One of these tests was the Porteus Mazes, which required the individual to trace with a pencil a path from a central point to an exit without going into a cul-de-sac. The mazes, which were graduated in difficulty, tested the individual's ability to plan, to be foresightful. The following question occurred to me: how could some of the youngsters I had tested manage to plan a runaway, sometimes very successfully, from a carefully supervised environment although they could not successfully do the simplest of mazes? The fact is that tests of mental ability rest on the unwarranted assumption that performance in contrived and naturally occurring situations are highly correlated. These tests were not developed on the basis of systematic observations of behavior in naturally occurring situations. If they had been, the test developers would have observed activities composed of processes—artistic activity and aesthetic response, for example—no less universal, no less humanly distinctive, no less a feature of human potential than the cognitive factors the developers riveted on. But that possibility could not be entertained as long as the test developers focused on what was required for an individual to perform adequately in the classroom.

That brings us to the third assumption, which concerned "special" abilities. The adjective *special* implied that certain mental processes and activities give rise to products or performances that are socially valuable. That is to say, they are special features of special individuals—children who display unusual artistic, musical, or literary ability. Frequently these individuals are labeled "gifted," indeed special, by virtue of either inborn factors or an unexplainable conjunction of cognitive and environmental factors. They possess cognitive factors that put them in a class by themselves.[1] That they are intelligent goes without saying, but it also goes without saying that they have something that is not encompassed by conventional conceptions of intelligence. And whatever that something is, it is not a universal feature of human potential. To include and measure that something by intelligence tests is to confuse the universal with the idiosyncratic.

There have always been critics of conventional conceptions of intelligence and intelligence tests. But it was not until the post–World War II era that those criticisms took on force and direction in two ways. The first was a challenge to the conceptual separation of intelligence and personality. How could one explain why individuals with similar and even identical intelligence test scores differed discernibly in the quality, effectiveness, and novelty-producing uses of their "intelligence"? Granted that intelligence tests predicted school performance well, why were they far less adequate for predicting the level and quality of problem-solving behavior outside the classroom? For example, over the years I have observed scores of classrooms containing either mentally retarded or "gifted" individuals. These tended to be small classes, and the teachers learned a lot about the students in and out of school. Regardless of the degree of homogeneity in test scores, every teacher was impressed by the variation in the uses of "intelligence" by these students in "real-life" arenas. Every teacher was similarly impressed by the variation in quality of use *in* the classroom. Both Johnny and Jimmy have IQs of 170, but, as one teacher said to me: "Johnny is really a dodo, he really doesn't or can't use what he has got, but Jimmy is a delight in that you cannot predict what question he will ask or what answer he will come up with." Another teacher put it this way: "I distinguish between intelligence and brightness. All of my students are highly intelligent on your tests, but your tests tell me nothing about who has that intellectual spark, that way of thinking that lightens what is usually a dull or ordinary day." No reader of this book will have difficulty coming up with similar observations and conclusions from life experience.

What gets illuminated when it is said that intelligence and personality cannot or should not be separated for theoretical and practical pur-

---

1. This point of view has been effectively criticized by David Feldman in his book *Nature's Gambit* (1986), based on intensive case studies of six prodigies. I summarize his critique and reconceptualization of the issue in chapter 10.

poses? Not very much, if only because the separation being challenged is maintained in our language. Intelligence is one "thing," "personality" is another, and the latter becomes an etiological factor to explain features of the former. "Brightness" is explained by personality, leaving "intelligence" as a concept pretty much what it was before, whereas the radical version of the challenge implies a unity obscured by language. As concepts, intelligence and personality are inventions to explain human thinking and behavior. As the etymology of the word implies, a concept is a creation, something new, a process distinctively human. But if we inevitably have or develop concepts, it is also the case that more often than not they distort or do violence to the phenomena they are intended to illuminate. And that is what has happened by keeping the concepts intelligence and personality separate and invoking each to explain aspects of the other.

This brings us to the second challenge to the conventional conception of intelligence and intelligence tests, which is wrapped up in the question: is not our concept of intelligence and intelligence tests blatantly deficient in ignoring or avoiding the attribute of creativity? The initial question is not whether people differ in the frequency and quality of creative activity—that can be taken for granted—but rather whether creativity is a universal human attribute. The strange fact is that this question has never occupied mainstream psychology. It is as if psychology agreed with the popular view that creativity is not normally distributed but rather a kind of all-or-nothing attribute that relatively few people possess. Psychologists, like others, have long been interested in those who have been obviously creative—Da Vinci, Galileo, Picasso, Einstein, Shakespeare. But however fascinating and important studies of such individuals are, their relevance to the development of a general psychology has been viewed as limited; they tell us a lot about a certain *kind* of individual, not about people generally.

For a short period in the post–World War II decades, creativity as a concept, and as a basis for criticizing narrow views of intelligence, became a focus of interest. If that interest was fleeting, it was because of what I term the "flight to measurement." What is creativity and how do we measure it? These are not, of course, trivial questions, but focusing on them had the effect of restricting observation of the phenomenon to schoolchildren and selected groups of adults. It is really incorrect to say "observation" if by this word we mean looking at the phenomenon in naturally occurring contexts. That is quite different from looking at it in contrived situations with predetermined categories of problems and judgment. It is not that one way is right and the other wrong; each has its time and place. But the flight to measurement had several untoward effects. The first was that it drew attention away from the central question: is creativity a normal human attribute? The second was that it did not lead to the observation of very young children or to an examination of the vast observational literature on children's play and problem solving. And the third was that it created a paradox: if creativity is indeed a human attribute observable in every young child, why does it seem to languish or disappear as the years pass and children go on to school?

If anything characterizes the very young child, it is curiosity about and responsiveness to stimuli in its internal and external contexts. The child is a seeking, active organism that is always impacting and impacted upon. The process is transactional in that the child's "inside and outside" are phenomenologically a unity; each is in the other, each is transformed in some way. The distinction that we as observers draw between stimulus and response does violence to the transactional nature of behavior. The inadequacies of the "reflex arc concept" were noted by John Dewey in 1896:

Let us take, for our example, the familiar child-candle instance. The ordinary interpretation would say the sensation of light is a stimulus to the grasping as a response, the burn resulting is a stimulus to withdrawing the hand as a response and so on. There is, of course, no doubt that is a rough practical way of representing the process. But when we ask for its psychological adequacy, the case is quite different. Upon analysis, we find that we begin not with a sensory stimulus, but with a sensorimotor coordination, the optical-ocular, and that in a certain sense it is the movement which is primary, and the sensation which is secondary, the movement of body, head and eye muscles determining the quality of what is experienced. *In other words, the real beginning is with the act of seeing; it is looking and not a sensation of light.* The sensory quale gives the value of the act, just as the movement furnishes its mechanism and control, but both sensation and movement lie inside, not outside, the act.

Now if this act, the seeing, stimulates another act, the reaching, it is because both of these acts fall within a larger co-ordination; because seeing and grasping have been so often bound together to reinforce each other, to help each other out, that each may be considered practically a subordinate member of a bigger co-ordination. More specifically, the ability of the hand to do its work will depend, either directly or indirectly, upon its control, as well as its stimulation, by the act of vision. If the sight did not inhibit as well as excite the reaching, the latter would be purely indeterminate, it would be for anything or nothing, not for the particular object seen. The reaching, in turn, must both stimulate and control the seeing. The eye must be kept upon the candle if the arm is to do its work; let it wander and the arm takes up another task. In other words, we now have an enlarged and transformed co-ordination; the act is seeing no less than before, but it is now seeing-for-teaching purposes. There is still a sensorimotor circuit, one with more content or value, not a substitution of a motor response for a sensory stimulus.[2]

In this seminally astounding paper, Dewey is doing more than putting flesh on the bones of the abstract stimulus-response explanation. He is emphasizing the active, questing role of the organism in its transactions with its surround. It is not a passive role; it is a transforming one, a role in which inside and outside are coordinated and changed. And it is this kind of transactional-change process that contains the seeds of what we call creativity: bringing about and producing something unique in the child's experience. Not all characterizations of the early years withstand close scrutiny, but this is not the case for the description of the developing child as one in whom awe and wonder about an unfolding world are omnipresent—not only awe and wonder about the world, but also about the changes the child brings about in that world.

It is hard to observe a child at play, even before the child can crawl or walk, and not be impressed by the expressions of interest, delight, and wonder the child shows to changes brought about by its own actions. Some have said that the very young child has something akin to delusions of grandeur because it understandably misinterprets its role in the changes it perceives or brings about. It is the causal center of its world. The wisdom of that explanation is in the emphasis given to transactions in which the child actively experiences something new that it seeks to re-experience, each re-experience containing another new feature. It has also been said that a repetition compulsion is a feature of early childhood. In terms of overt behavior, that is probably valid. But the pathology (potential or not) connoted by the term *repetition compulsion* should not distract us from recognizing what is less obvious and crucially significant: the reinforcement these repetitions give to the sense of mastery, the sense that one can control and alter something "out there." That sense of mastery and alteration, of molding and transforming, that sense of struggle and satisfaction from a product "out there" that is isomorphic in some way with imagery "inside"—those are the embryonic features of the creative process and its products. I use the word *product* because it emphasizes the active, purposeful role of the very young producer. To

2. *The Psychological Review* 1896: 357–80.

the adult observer, that product may have no recognizable form or significance, thereby putting the emphasis on some internal state and avoiding the necessity of labeling what appears to be unamenable to labeling. When we say the child is playing, we recognize its internal, imaginative features and gloss over the fact that the child is seeking to transform the outside congruently with internal imagery and feeling. We would think it odd and inappropriate to assert that this very young child is engaging in an artistic activity. That says more about how we have been taught to define artistic activity than about the origins and development of that activity.

Young children, regardless of their society and its culture, produce a change "out there" whose visual significance stimulates them to continue the activity. The medium used may be a pencil, paint, sand, or any other plastic material. We call the product "scribbles" and the process "scribbling" to indicate two things: the lack of a recognizable form and the seemingly random and uncoordinated nature of the child's movements. We do not say that the activity is purposeless because it is obvious that in continuing the activity the child is experiencing some kind of satisfaction. So we are likely to say that the child continues the activity because it is deriving some kind of bodily pleasure from its movements. But when we say that, we are ignoring the transactions between what the child *sees* it has done and what it continues to do. Like Dewey's description of the child reaching for the lighted candle, the scribbles begin with and are a bodily response to the visual. But unlike the child who reaches for and touches the lighted candle, the child "producer" continues the visually guided activity. When we observe that young child over a period of weeks and months, the scribbles become less amorphous, a recognizable circle begins to appear, and not too long after that the circle becomes more differentiated, a sequence noted countless times by observers of young children in scores of widely differing societies.[3]

For my purposes the significance of that progression is not in what it suggests about the developmental process—that is, how it is characterized by stages reflecting growth in "mental structures or schemas" and sensorimotor coordinations. The significance of that progression, I wish to emphasize, is what it says about the emergence of artistic form: a

---

3. Someone once said that in the case of the young child, Descartes' "I think, therefore I am" should be "I scribble, therefore I am"—i.e., that the act of scribbling is already an act of formation *and* transformation.

product, *however simple,* the parts of which are integrally related so that changing one of them (for example, its direction) destroys the impression of a visual unity. Although it is appropriate to say that it is a progression in which artistic form emerges, it is no less appropriate to say that it contains in embryonic form all the features of the creative process: transforming the "out there" in ways that bear the stamp of the producer. It is not a process the child engages in for the hell of it. It is an active, motivated activity exploiting the creative capabilities of the child at a particular stage of its development.

Artistic activity is not an "ability" that some children have and others do not. It is a universal attribute observable in all young children. As long as we think of the visual productions of young children as only a form of play, or as an exercise in coordination of movements, or as a kind of inchoate expressiveness, we will continue to gloss over the creative process of which those productions are consequences. We are so used to regarding artistic activity in relation to a small group of more mature people whom we call artists that we cannot recognize the kinship between them and young children. For example, when we describe the visual art of children as a kind of recreational play, we are implying that it is associated with a nonserious, semi-unreflective, very fluid process hardly under cognitive control, with few or no boundaries or intervals between steps in the process. But is that "playing around" completely dissimilar to the process engaged in by the mature artist whose sketches and drawings preliminary to painting so frequently appear to be an indulgence of child-like spontaneity? As one artist said to me (I paraphrase): "My earliest sketches for a painting are a deliberate playing around, a way of avoiding coming to quick closure, as free a way as possible of getting something on paper that begins to tell me what the artistic problem may be. When I sketch—and I love the feeling of freedom I experience when I sketch—I am not like the person who wants to climb Mt. Everest because it is there. I sketch because I do not know what is there until I put it there and can look at it and then do another sketch. It is not that I regress to the level of the child. I never feel more creative than when I am sketching."

I once observed a young child, no more than a year of age, whose mother had planted her on wet sand a couple of yards away from a receding ocean tide. For a minute or so she scanned the water, the small waves, and older children nearby. She then looked at her hands, in each of which was a clump of wet sand that trickled through her fingers. She seemed fascinated by the trickling sand and then began vigorously to scoop up more sand and follow its downward course. She would stop, visually examining the holes she had made and the tiny mounds the trickling sand had formed. Then she would scoop up more sand and again watch its descent, occasionally riveting on the many mounds around her.

We do not think about these kinds of observation in terms of creativity or artistic activity because we have so overlearned the habit of applying those terms to recognizable products or forms. We look at the end product, and if it appears to have no apparent configuration we conclude that the process that gave rise to it has no configurative properties or special developmental significance or reflective attributes that should be nurtured. And yet, no student of early development has ever asserted that the seeds and flowering of creativity and artistic activity are not attributes that all young children manifest in some way at some time or many times. Despite this affirmation, research on and observations of artistic activity as a manifestation of creativity have been far from the mainstream of the field. If one were forced briefly to characterize the developmental literature, it would not be inappropriate to say that its main thrust has been to describe and understand the origins, nature, and emergence of logical thinking, the young child as budding scientist. The portrait of the young child as embryonic artist has hardly been sketched; the significance of artistic activity as a universal attribute has hardly been discussed or formulated.

It is, I trust, clear that I regard artistic activity as a series of coordinated bodily (eye-hand) movements that transforms, or creates a change in, some aspect of the configurated "out there" that is satisfying and motivating so that the child persists in the activity, each new attempt producing some perceptible change in the configuration. The products are configurated and the process from which they emerge is configuring. The product is literally a creation. The product and the process are quite the opposite of random affairs. In the course of the activity, both undergo change in a transactional way.

As soon as one accepts artistic activity as a universal attribute of childhood, as a quintessentially creative activity, several questions have to be raised. The first has to do with the extent to which children differ in the frequency with which they display such activity. The question, I must emphasize, is not whether some children display the activity and others do not, but rather how one understands individual variations. That question, of course, will have many possible answers if only because we know that the contexts in which such activity can be displayed vary dramatically in social, interpersonal, motivating, material-media ways that can elicit, reinforce, or extinguish the activity.

So, for example, the child whose parents are artists or have a strong interest in art is in a very different context than the child whose parents have no interest in or knowledge of artistic activity. The child who lives in a context utterly devoid of any usable plastic medium has fewer opportunities to display artistic activity than the child bombarded with such media. We are all familiar with parents who place such a high value on early speech and reading that they create and take advantage of any opportunity to stimulate and support "readiness." If the possible explanations for individual differences in artistic activity are predictably legion, we can assume that an activity that has no developmental significance for the adults in the child's social context will not be nurtured. What we do in regard to a child's activity depends on the meanings and the future significances that activity has for us.

The fact is that most adults in our society do not see children as embryonic artists. If, as I have, you read scores of popular books on child rearing, you will be hard put to find a suggestion that children engage in artistic activity, whose developmental significance is no less momentous than learning to read or use numbers. You will find discussions about the importance of stimulating and supporting the child's expressiveness, avoiding actions that can stifle curiosity, question asking, and imaginativeness. But those discussions are directed to "personality" organization and development, not to the development of artistic activity and the creation of artistic form and products. So, for example, finger paints are recommended as a means for untrammeled emotional expressiveness, a kind of bodily catharsis, and not as an opportunity for, or step in, producing and responding to artistic form and color. Anyone who observes a young child beginning to finger paint will be impressed by the child's seeming delight with its experience of the fluids and fluid movements. The observer is likely to ignore the role of the child's *visual* interest in what it has produced in the "out there." To us, what the child has produced has "no form." This conclusion is nonsensical given the fact that visual perception always involves a form and a ground, a fact that in recent years has been demonstrated in neonates. Indeed, if you watch over a period of minutes a child who has begun to finger paint, you will find that the visual component of the configurated activity becomes more obvious and even dominant.

As process and product, artistic activity characterizes the young child. Why does such an assertion strike most people as oxymoronic?

What is there about our conception of creativity and artistic activity that makes it virtually impossible to observe and consider the young child as embryonic artist? Is it that our conception of what is art and non-art is so focused on product that we ignore the process? Is the difficulty we have in seeing the child as embryonic artist a consequence of the vague intuition that if we change our view, we would not know what practical actions we should take, where such a change could lead us? Or is it that we cannot overcome the belief that artistic activity is a special ability with which some people have been blessed? Or is it, generally speaking, that we are captive to the view that ignores the fact that the content and process of any activity are always in some ways suffused with a world-view derived from culture, ideology, and history?

There are myriads of perspectives from which we can view the sweep of human history. The one most relevant to my purposes is that which starts with the observation that history is distinguished by the ways in which the capacities of people have been vastly underestimated; more specifically, how in each past era the dominant ruling groups—be their power base economic, military, political, religious, or intellectual—looked upon those "below" them as inferior in some way, as lacking the potential to be "above" the crowd. Slaves were incapable of enjoying and productively using freedom. The "masses" were incapable of as-suming responsibility for wise actions; they were by nature followers, not leaders. Women were not only different from men, they were in-ferior to them. Imperial powers, east or west, were justifiably imperial in light of the primitive and barbaric customs of those they subjugated, ruled, and treated as less than human. Formal education, however defined, required abilities that only a few possessed. And children, very young children, were unformed and unforming organisms born in original sin and, therefore, requiring persistent indoctrination and control. They were things and objects, devoid of the characteristics of "people."

Examples of man's underestimation of man are legion in human history. Today, we like to believe that we have overcome this tendency and are open to the suggestion that we have underestimated the devel-opmental potential of people. It is one thing to say that we are more sensitive than those in the past to the tendency to underestimate; it is illusory to say that we have overcome it. Like those in the past, we have a worldview grounded in axioms that, by the very nature of axioms, seem so right, natural, and proper that we never formulate them or put them into words. We assimilate and accept our worldview, and we do not think about it unless events force us to do so. Little on the current societal scene forces us to consider the possibility that we vastly underestimate artistic activity as a universal human attribute. Why we do so, and why we should examine this tendency as a way of illuminating our society and world-view, are the major foci of this book. What is at stake is not only how we regard what people are but also what they potentially can be. Obviously, I say that in a positive sense: I mean what people can *desirably* be. In this century we have been witness to people and events—the Holocaust, the Armenian massacre, Hitler, Stalin, the Chinese Cultural Revolution, Khomeini—that speak volumes about what people are and can be. In some abstract sense we know that people have the potential to commit unforgivable actions of such dimensions as to overwhelm our capacity to comprehend. At the same time we know that we feel impotent, as individuals or nations, to stop—let alone prevent—such actions. But at least a part of us knows that the concept of human potential has its dark side. If this book is about the bright side, I do not expect that it will be any easier to comprehend than the dark side. If it should turn out to be easier to comprehend, the revolution that comprehension suggests for the ways we think and the thrust of our educational institutions will not be warmly embraced. Worldviews, as they are reflected in our daily lives and societal institutions, change slowly.

3 ◆ THE UNFOLDING OF

ARTISTIC ACTIVITY

The title of this chapter is also the title of a book by Henry Schaefer-Simmern, a man who influenced and altered my thinking in countless ways. I met him in 1942, shortly after I took a position as psychologist at the Southbury (Connecticut) Training School for mentally retarded individuals. He was a political refugee from Hitler's Germany, where he had already become known as an artist, art theorist, and art educator. In my autobiography *The Making of an American Psychologist* (1988), I devoted a long chapter to Schaefer-Simmern in which I describe the development of our intellectual and personal relationship. He was the most extraordinary person I have ever known. Here I shall not go into what Schaefer-Simmern was like as a person and why, despite the disparity in our ages, our relationship was so vital to each of us. I shall restrict myself to his ideas, what they meant in practice, and what he enabled people, truly "ordinary" people, to produce as artists.[1]

It is not happenstance that the foreword of Schaefer-Simmern's *Unfolding of Artistic Activity* was one of the last things John Dewey wrote. If Schaefer-Simmern's ideas and work concerned artistic activity in ordinary people, he was no ordinary mortal.

Precisely because of Schaefer-Simmern's ideas, I cannot begin this account without saying something about the Southbury Training School as a work of art. We are not used to thinking about and judging a complex set of physical structures, especially a state institution, as a work of art, an embodiment of a process in which external features and internal imagery are in constant transaction, culminating ultimately in the physical scene we perceive. To most such scenes we hardly have a reaction; there is nothing to arrest the eye, nothing to which we react. If forced to react, we might say that the structure is nondescript, that it

1. Schaefer-Simmern is the subject of a soon-to-be-completed doctoral dissertation by Raymond C. Berta at the Stanford University School of Education.

has no distinguishing features reflective of a creative process. And in rendering that judgment we are unaware that we may be misinterpreting the process because of our nonaffective response to the product. Just as the scribbles or finger painting of a young child are gratuitously judged as reflective of a chaotic mental-bodily process, having no configurated or configuring properties, we conclude that the nondescript structure we are forced to judge is the outcome of a noncreative, nonartistic process.

I am sure that there are times when such a judgment is appropriate, as when the structure is obviously a copy of other structures. I am no less certain that if we studied the process that gave rise to such a structure we would not find it devoid of the creative artistic process. This does not mean, of course, that because in these instances the processes have certain features in common, we should especially value their products. What it does mean is that we should not confuse product and process or, at the least, that we should be aware that going from product to process is no simple affair. Rather, it is at every step suffused with culturally determined judgments about what is art and non-art, what is good and bad art. By treating it as a simple affair we cannot even entertain the possibility that artistic activity is a universal human attribute.

But each of us has had the experience of seeing a structure or structures that are arresting to the eye and compel our attention. Our spontaneous reaction may be positive or negative, and we are content, for the most part, not to go beyond expressions of liking and disliking. And that is the point: we are so schooled to stop at our spontaneous or affective response, so riveted on the product, that we find it odd that the processes culminating in things we like and dislike can have common features. This seems as improbable as the assertion that the very young child is an embryonic artist, a creative organism. When we like any work of art, regardless of the reasons, we find it "natural" to regard it as creative. When we dislike a work of art, it is quite another story.

When I first saw the Southbury Training School in 1942, I thought we had taken a wrong road and come upon a most beautiful college campus. It was the right road, the school had opened several months before, and I was to be interviewed for a position. In the several years I was there I never met anyone who, seeing it for the first time, did not respond with awe and wonder to the scene. It was arresting! However, like all the others', my appreciation stopped with expressions of delight. It did not occur to me that what I saw was a creative work of art, the result of a long, complex process during which there were ever-changing transactions between internal imagery and goals on the one hand, and an external topography on the other hand. I responded in a spontaneous, non-analytic way to a "product," totally insensitive to and ignorant of the conceptual and personal turmoil accompanying those transactions. Was it a work of art? If pressed I would have assented to the proposition that the product reflected a high degree of creativity—that Southbury as a visual scene was unique among such residential institutions, public or private.

But uniqueness is not the hallmark of creativity or of a work of art. I would have agreed that Southbury was a work of art, but reluctantly, because to me art was in museums. I was unschooled to recognize that the process from which Southbury had emerged was no different from the process that gave rise to what was housed in museums. I was a victim of the pervasive cultural and educational bias that not only told us what was art and where we could find it, but rendered us conceptually blind to the countless ways in which people engage in artistic activity. So, for example, if I saw a garden I thought was pretty or beautiful, it would never have occurred to me that it was a product of the artistic process, that my affective response was to something that had form, something that was the opposite of a random configuration of form and color. Of course, I would have said, Southbury had a form that somehow *informed* my response to it, a response that I daily experienced. But what were the characteristics of that form? I would not have been capable of an answer precisely because I had no knowledge of the artistic process, how form is created and recreated in the tug-of-war among internal imagery, medium, and the "out there." I was oblivious to the fact that if the appearance or placement or direction of any of the structures comprising the institution had been altered, it would have introduced a jarring note into one's visual perception of the totality.

Who is an artist? In a cultural-sociological sense we do not answer that question in terms of the presence or absence of the artistic process but rather in terms of product, role, or label. We do not think of the person who creates a lovely garden as an artist. Similarly, when we see a fruit and vegetable store that gains our attention by the color and form of the arrangement of its produce, we would not say that the arranger is an artist. Or when we walk into someone's home and react with delight to what we visually perceive, we are unlikely to say that the person who conceived the scene is an artist.

In this cultural-sociological sense, Southbury was not created by an artist. That is, Mr. Roselle, the superintendent of Southbury, was not an artist. He was given many labels: educator, administrator, salesman, entrepreneur, and frustrated architect. It was his internal vision that got transformed into what we saw. Of course, professional architects had the responsibility for developing the structures. Mr. Roselle was not a consultant to them; they were in his service. If he knew precious little about mental retardation, an endless source of criticism and humor, he knew in a most encompassing way what he wanted South-bury to look like.

When I walked into his office, the first thing I saw was a mural-sized topographical, scaled drawing of the institution: the existing and future structures. To this audience of one he explained why he had planned Southbury as it appeared, why this building was here and that one there, and when and why future structures would be built. He hardly interviewed me for the position I sought. I sat there nonplused. He lived in a visual world, I lived in a world of abstractions. He lived in a world of forms and colors, I lived in a world of ideas. I was a psychologist, but what was Mr. Roselle? Labels may be linguistic conveniences, indeed necessities, but too often we forget that they imply a conception of human behavior and capacity that obscures as much as it may illuminate. Mr. Roselle was an artist who in creating Southbury as a visual form remade himself and his world. It was not that he had a "special" gift but rather that I (we) had the narrowest conception of who is an artist and what is artistic activity.

It is not happenstance, of course, that when Mr. Roselle was asked by the Russell Sage Foundation to provide the facilities for Henry Schaefer-Simmern to demonstrate artistic development in mentally retarded individuals, he enthusiastically assented. I have no doubt that if that request had been made of the superintendent of every comparable institution in this country, the negative replies would have been unanimous, and on two grounds. First, they could not justify freeing space for such a project. Second, on the face of it, it was ridiculous to talk seriously about artistic activity in institutionalized, mentally retarded individuals. It would be more correct to say mentally retarded *children* because, regardless of chronological age, that is what the residents were called. To talk about artistic activity or creativity in such individuals was really too much, another example of ignorance or misguided utopianism or a squandering of money better used elsewhere.

Mr. Roselle asked me to help Schaefer-Simmern in whatever ways were necessary. When I first met Schaefer-Simmern my heart sank, because I believed that his heavily accented speech would frequently be mystifying to the residents. Also, his manner and mien struck me as typically Prussian: he rarely smiled, and he seemed deadly serious to a degree that could intimidate the residents (as it did me, initially). It was immediately obvious that Schaefer-Simmern was incapable of small talk, and I quickly asked him if he would tell me what he was about and what kinds and numbers of residents he needed. He told me the following:

1. All human beings are capable of artistic activity. The seeds of that activity are already discernible in the earliest scribbles of children and in the orderly progression of artistic form as the child develops in that activity.

2. The child has no intention of copying reality or reproducing something from memory. The child intends a form, a product, that is congruent with or a reflection of a visual conception: an internal creation or "picture" that is the child's reality.

3. No mature artist intends or tries to copy nature. Even if the artist wanted to, he or she could not do it. The artist transforms the "out there" in line with a visual conception that is unique to that artist at a particular stage of development. The artist, child or adult, seeks to see out there what he sees inside. And what he sees inside is not a copy of reality.

4. Nothing in Western society more effectively subverts and extinguishes artistic activity than the judgment that the artistic product should be a copy of reality, a product of "memory." That judgment has virtually blinded us to the creative capacity of people, especially in our schools, where children are required to imitate reality. Is it any wonder that they grow up to see themselves as uncreative?

5. There are numerous media through which artistic activity is or can be manifest. There are societies, past and present, in which all members engage in artistic activity. They are not troubled or intimidated by such questions as who is an artist and what is a work of art. They do what they do, they make what they make, as part of a familiar pattern of mental and social activity.

6. Artistic activity is far more than the phrase "personal expression" suggests. It is an ordered activity through which product and creator are constantly being changed, each undergoing more and more differentiation.

7. To the extent that people are "educated" to regard themselves as uncreative, the satisfactions they experience in regard to artistic ac-

tivity, either as agents or as aesthetic observers, are diminished and their development in general is impoverished.

8. For two decades Schaefer-Simmern had worked with ordinary individuals (young and old, educated and not, skilled and unskilled workers) whose artistic development and products surprised them and everyone else. Although the artistic development of all of them, in terms of the progression of form, had features in common, the work of each bore a distinctive, indeed unique, imprint.

9. Schaefer-Simmern wanted to demonstrate that institutionalized, mentally retarded "children" could develop as artists, just as he had, he said, demonstrated with institutionalized juvenile delinquents.

With one exception, I truly did not comprehend what Schaefer-Simmern said. I had no knowledge or experience to help me put his statements into any meaningful context. Art was foreign territory to me. Indeed, the idea that I was capable of artistic activity was ridiculous. That it was a universal attribute was laughable. That it was an activity in which retarded individuals could meaningfully and productively engage was an indulgence of utopian thinking. The exception was that by background and political ideology I cottoned to a man who said that we underestimate the potential of people. In short, I wanted to believe Schaefer-Simmern was right at the same time that I had to conclude he was egregiously wrong.

Schaefer-Simmern requested that I arrange for him to meet ten or so residents who were representative of the run-of-the-mill, physically normal Southbury population. He would see them individually in my office, and he would then select six of them to work in the "studio" space Mr. Roselle had given to him. When he returned to Southbury the next week, the residents and I were waiting for him.

I brought them in one at a time. I stayed in the office to observe and to be of any assistance, and I expected that my assistance would be needed. With each resident Schaefer-Simmern began by asking for the person's name and requesting that he or she draw something with the paper and pencil he offered. He was interested, he said, in what they drew and how they drew it. What immediately struck me was how his manner with each resident communicated interest in what that person would do. It would be more appropriate to say he manifested a serious respect for whatever each would do. Although his manner was soft and respectful, he never smiled, he was all business, and he warmly thanked each of them for acceding to his request. My assistance was never needed.

I do not remember how I selected those residents, but it was in a semirandom way. Two of them were known in the institution for their flowing, florid drawings which, to me, were strangely disquieting. The others, all female, were truly run-of-the-mill "high-grade" mentally retarded individuals who had been in institutions for a decade or more and were quiet and docile, truly unremarkable. Except for Selma, who was retarded and schizophrenic, who slaved away in the laundry, never had a visitor, and whose case folder contained every type of child abuse. Selma was regarded as mystifying, queer, pathetic, but likable in the way one likes an obedient, dependent, faithful old dog.

After the last of the residents had left, Schaefer-Simmern studied their products very carefully. On what basis, I asked, was he going to select? He sorted the drawings into two piles, put them before me, and said that he had selected pile A. I was taken aback because pile B struck me as more "artistic" by far than pile A, which to my eye contained primitive drawings, such as simple stick figures. Pointing to the pile he had rejected, Schaefer-Simmern said: "These drawings are products of memory, attempts to copy reality. They did not draw what they could see, what would be in accord with a visual conception, but what was an imitation of what they thought they *should* draw. They have been *spoiled.* As a result, they drew what is essentially a visual chaos that is a result of trying to copy nature. The drawings in the other pile are very, very simple but have, nevertheless, artistic form: a gestalt, a configuration in which you cannot make a change without altering the form in a way that would be visually distracting to us. They drew what they could see, their visual conception, their internal reality."

For Schaefer-Simmern, analyzing a work of art began and ended with the "visual data." In his dissertation on Schaefer-Simmern, Ray Berta (1990) emphasizes this point by relating an incident contained in an interview with Rudolf Arnheim, who was a personal and intellectual friend of Schaefer-Simmern:

> During the late 1950s with a group of prominent Bay Area women in the Atherton home of Elise Stern Haas, Arnheim recalls a woman new to the group presenting her first painting to HSS for analysis. She began, "Professor Schaefer-Simmern, there is a great deal *behind* my painting." The woman alluded to some psychological interpretation or meaning *behind* her painting. Arnheim, knowing full well HSS's pristine dedication to "visual facts only" and his aversion to any type of psychological reading into art, enjoyed watching HSS carefully lift her painting, turn it over with great flourish, study the blank back side meticulously, and then dramatically an-

nounce: "Oh? Is there something *behind* your painting? Madame, I do not see anything *behind* but raw canvas and a wood frame. In order to understand art, we don't have to wonder what's *behind* it. Everything is there in the front on the canvas, not *behind* the canvas. Please remember there is nothing more factual than a work of art. We have only to open our eyes and see the visual relationships. These visual facts constitute artistic form, nothing else. Please do not believe a single word I say about artistic form unless I can prove it to you with visual facts only."

Schaefer-Simmern understood well that a work of art could be studied from different perspectives or interests—art-historical, psycho-historical, cultural, and so on. However legitimate these perspectives may be, they could not and should not be substitutes for studying and understanding how a work of art is configured and the degree to which parts hang, so to speak, together. It is the cognitive processes of configuring that are so uniquely human, however simple that configuring may seem to be. It is a configuring not only of the "out there" but of the maker's "in here." The maker "becomes" no less than the work of art "becomes." Form forms. That is why Schaefer-Simmern could not abide imitation and that is why, as Berta documents, he was not only the most articulate critic of customary art education but became a persona non grata on that scene.

Let us listen to Schaefer-Simmern describe complicated works of art. The quotations (1966) are taken from taped lectures he gave at St. Mary's College in Moraga, California.

> This painting is Piero di Cosimo's *Simonetta Vespucci,* painted about 1495. The artistic form in this portrait is built upon one problem, namely, the borderless transition from figure to ground between light and dark shapes. Every dark shape relates to its neighboring light shape. The dark cloud behind and to the left of Simonetta's profile brings out her face in a monumental way. The light cloud behind and to the right of her head brings out the complexity and differentiation in her dark hair. This cloud cannot be dark because her hair is also dark. Look at her nose, arm, and shoulder. They are all set against dark grounds. Look at her breast. Exactly the same—light, dark. The inside of her dark shawl brings out her light upper body. The dark outside of the entire shawl sets against the lighter ground of the landscape and sky. Here artistic form consists mainly of the highly intelligent application of figure/ground relationships where the figure meaning in one shape gradually passes into the ground meaning in a neighboring shape and vice versa.

> This painting is Gudron Egeberg's *Negro Boy Sitting in Morningside Park with Harlem in the Background,* painted in 1942. The boy's figure embodies the

principal meaning of the whole picture. This effect is intensified by the sharp contrast among the colors in the figure and the background. The contrast is produced by the figure/ground relationship of his dark brown head against the light yellow-green evening sky, by his white shirt against the dark reddish-brown complex of the houses, by his intensely red-orange shorts against the light gray surface of the rocks on which the boy is sitting, and finally, by his dark brown legs, red-orange stockings, and black shoulder against the light gray side view of the rock.

I close my lecture by showing the mental meaning of lines organized into figure/ground relationships in a drawing by Albrecht Dürer. Dürer drew *Peasant Couple Dancing* in 1514. The couple dance against a clear white background. Their arms, legs, and torsos coalesce into a single pinwheel-shaped structure. The man's back serves as ground for the woman's figure because Dürer's artistic idea is a couple dancing, not a separate man and woman. Each and every zigzag or curving line varies or repeats the circular quality of the total form. Look how the lines in the man's arms curve into the woman's arms and then cavort down and up and around each of their legs. These lines sweep them off their feet. Different figure/ground relationships in each arm and leg suggest the rhythm and vitality of their dance. Here you cannot change a single line, stroke, or dot without destroying the unity of their dance. Suddenly we see and understand Dürer's mind. His formal organization of lines into complex figure/ground relationships reflects the essence of his mental being. Consequently, this drawing becomes nothing else than a manifestation of Dürer's mind.

(Egeberg's painting is the frontispiece of Schaefer-Simmern's book, and I have reproduced it as figure 24; it also appears in color on the dust jacket of this book.) There is an identity between what Schaefer-Simmern has said and what Samuel Lipman said in the brief passage I quoted in chapter 1.

Language may be the best means of communication we have, but it is inadequate for describing an artistic product or an artistic development. Therefore, before discussing further Schaefer's ideas and pedagogical approach, I shall reproduce samples of what came out of the "studio" and of the work of others with whom Schaefer-Simmern had worked.[2]

Let us begin with Selma, who was thirty years old:

She had an I.Q. of 49, which means that she was on the borderline between imbecile and moron. She had never attended regular school. At the time of

2. I am grateful to the University of California Press for permission to reproduce illustrations and text from *The Unfolding of Artistic Activity*.

her admission to an institution for mental defectives she had only attended special classes. She showed little inclination to learn and was reported by her teachers to be "lazy and indifferent." At the time of her entrance into the Southbury Training School she was "unresponsive, inarticulate, and phlegmatic." She was sloppy, fat, unattractive in appearance, and had a vague empty stare. Her response to all questions consisted of a shake of her head or a groan. She would obey a direct command, she never caused any trouble or disturbance, but she showed absolutely no initiative in making friends or social contacts. She would prefer to withdraw to the fringe of a crowd and be a spectator and never a participant in cottage activities.

When the writer met her for the first time, she gave an impression of being very shy. It was difficult to have a conversation with her because she answered reluctantly and in monosyllables. When unoccupied she seemed very restless and unhappy and would walk through the workshop talking to herself. Now, in order to determine a person's stage of visual conception, the author generally asks him to draw whatever he wishes. From a person of Selma's mental level any spontaneous creative activity could hardly be expected. For this reason she was not required to draw something of her own choice. Furthermore, it would have been impossible for her to respond to a sudden request that demanded quick decision; in fact, had she thus been called upon, it might have endangered her emotional equilibrium. In order to stimulate her, the author showed her a drawing done by a seven-year-old child, since it could be expected that her stage of development of visual conception would correspond to that of a normal child of approximately the same mental age as her own. It would seem reasonable to suppose that she could only grasp others' pictures that were in conformity with the stage of visual conception which she had already reached. Obviously she was able to react to the clearcut, outlined picture since she found it "very pretty" [fig. 1]. After she had observed it for about ten minutes, it was removed and she was asked to make something similar in her own way. She was given a piece of paper 10 by 14 inches in size and an oil crayon. She started to work immediately and finished her drawing in twenty minutes.

When she was requested to show her work, her feelings of inferiority, her shyness, and even a certain anxiety gripped her. Turning her face away, she submitted her drawing with trembling hands. She obviously feared attention and criticism.

Her picture represents trees and flowers, with air, sky and sun above [fig. 2]. It has a subject similar to that of the drawing shown her, because trees and flowers are also the main content of that drawing. Furthermore, the structural order is almost the same; each single object stands by itself and is determined in its vertical direction by a horizontal base line. The forms of the trees are also visualized, as in the sample picture, by variability of direction. But in spite of all these points of likeness, Selma's drawing is by no means a copy of the picture shown. The similarity exists in the stage of development

Fig. 1. Drawing by a seven-year-old child.

Fig. 2. Selma's first drawing, done with colored crayon.

of visual conception. The peculiarity in the forms of the trees, their parallel arrangement, the long, horizontal base line by which the whole drawing attains a clear order, bring out the difference in the individual application of this stage of development. Irrespective of how crude and simple the drawing may appear, it must be recognized as showing independence of visual conception.

Selma's first picture—according to her own statement, the only one she had ever done—already indicates that even a mentally deficient person can create in a modest degree an ordered pictorial whole.

It was astonishing that she was able to accomplish even so simple a pictorial result, and the writer praised her for her work. Her reserved attitude disappeared at once, and a big smile spread over her face; apparently, a word of encouragement was what she needed. Another fact was still more astonishing. While the writer was engaged in supervising the work of the other girls belonging to the same group, Selma took some drawing paper from the desk and started a new picture [fig. 3]. She repeated almost the same subject. She placed in the center a large tree surrounded by smaller trees, on a long, wavy base line. Parallel to the base line, another line forms the lower border of the sky, which is colored blue, and the sun is in the right-hand part of the sky. Except for a little more careful execution of her drawing, there is no further development in the organization of form. But two essential facts must be noted: the smaller trees show a different application of the stage of variability of direction of lines, a variation of form invented by herself; and furthermore, the fact that she drew this picture spontaneously indicated the possibility of an unfolding of energies that no one had expected. (Pp. 33–36)

Three things are noteworthy here. The first is Schaefer-Simmern's sensitivity to the kind of person Selma was. To my knowledge she is the only resident for whom he thought it necessary to facilitate a beginning by showing her someone else's product. Schaefer was no psychologist who reacted to a resident in terms of diagnostic labels, such as mentally retarded or schizophrenic. Selma clearly stood apart from all the others, and he started with her differently. The second noteworthy fact is Schaefer-Simmern's attention to form, to figure-ground relationships, to the principle that seemed to govern interrelationships among lines. He studied Selma's pictures in no way differently than if they were those of a more artistically developed individual. The third thing, and in some ways the most illuminating of Schaefer-Simmern as teacher and theorist, is how he caught the fact that in her second drawing "the smaller trees show a different application of the stage of variability of direction of lines, a variation of form invented by herself." He saw

Fig. 3. Selma's second drawing.

change, however small, that ordinarily escapes notice. For example, in relation to her third drawing (fig. 4), Schaefer-Simmern tells us:

> With the suggestion that she proceed slowly and carefully, Selma went to work. She spent almost an hour in the execution of her third drawing. The picture again represents a familiar content. Three trees are placed on a wavy base line. The space between the lower edge of the sheet of paper and the base line is filled in with green; obviously, that color carries the meaning of hills. The lower edge forms the horizontal base for five large flowers colored a darker green. As in her second picture, the upper line marking the sky is drawn parallel to the base line. The distinct construction of the whole drawing and the more careful execution reveal that Selma is able to achieve an accurate performance when she is really interested in her subject, and when this performance is suited to the stage of her mental development; in other

Fig. 4. Selma's third drawing.

words, when she can fully grasp what she is doing. Under such conditions, her drive for visual clearness impels her to a clear pictorial realization which serves as an impetus for the development of new pictorial ideas. The result is to be seen in the formation of the trees. Whereas in the earlier drawings she differentiated the branches either by simple dots or strokes, she now applies both in a rhythmic order representing blossoms and leaves. Within this rhythmic order the various colors find their best application. They become an essential factor in the pictorial structure. Each tree now has different colors for its blossoms, whereby they are clearly distinguished from one another. The tree on the right side has red leaves and green blossoms, which indicates that for Selma color has primarily a structural function and is not used as a faithful reproduction of nature.

Selma's creative activity may appear to many observers as insignificant. But these tiny signs of creativeness become of great importance if they concern individuals who are usually thought of as creatively sterile. Although the results achieved will always, in terms of normal potentialities, remain comparatively modest, their effect upon the feeble-minded producer may be of decisive consequence.

For the next three months Selma's work could best be described as repetitive, as rigid:

After weeks of such "repetitions," Selma still made the same dots and strokes for blossoms and leaves. One day, almost three months after her beginning the course, all her drawings were shown to her in the sequence of their production. The ensuing conversation brought Selma to a clearer observation of those dots and strokes for blossoms and leaves. When asked if she were able to draw these parts "better," she expressed signs of instant confusion. She walked off, wandered through the workshop several times, and returned to say a shy "No." However, when she was advised to enlarge her trees on a larger sheet of paper so that she could see the single parts more clearly, she hesitatingly started to draw and tried to cover the whole sheet. But as she was used to another size of paper, she had to calculate visually the proportions of her new drawing. The problem placed her in extreme difficulties. Her struggle found an outlet in groans which indicated her desperate situation. She was so excited that her breath came shorter and faster. Yet she did not stop in her attempt. She tried it over and over again until she could organize her new drawing of a tree on the larger sheet of paper.

Selma's vigorous endeavor to find "better" shapes for her blossoms and leaves resulted in the formation of new pictorial elements [fig. 5]. The simple dots previously used to represent blossoms are now given the shape of circles. Three of them, carrying the meaning of petals, surround a central circle as the center of a blossom; within this new formation, Selma again applies her previous conception of form—a single round dot. As with the blossoms, so with the leaves; instead of single strokes, large circles determine their shape,

Fig. 5. After almost three months, Selma worked out new shapes for blossoms and leaves.

also. This progress may seem unimportant. However, when present in a mental defective with a low I.Q., it must be recognized as a positive factor in the free unfolding of ordered energies.

In all her earlier pictures Selma creates a definite organization in the relationship of the objects one to another. Trees and flowers are attached to their ground, the horizontal base line, in a vertical way which is the greatest contrast of direction to the ground. By this device the entire drawing receives an ordered stability. In spite of the fact that some details, such as branches, show a more advanced relationship of variability of direction with respect to the trunks, as soon as Selma faces a greater complex of objects, she regresses to the preceding stage of visual conception—the relationship of the horizontal-vertical. It has already been pointed out that this regression to an earlier stage follows a natural law. It can be found in all epochs, in the pictorial activity of primitive tribes, of children, and in genuine folk art.

For the purpose of stimulating Selma to a greater application of her creative abilities, the idea of a large complex of objects was brought to her notice. She was asked if she had ever seen a pond. Raising her voice—a sign of interest—she said, "Do you mean a pond with fish?" To this she received the answer: "Yes. Let's make a picture of such a pond and put your trees around it." She welcomed the suggestion and went to work immediately. She made a small drawing of a rectangular pond and put the trees around it, each big tree accompanied by a small tree. The outline of the pond became the horizontal base, and the trees were vertically directed from it all the way round. Selma intended to make the large trees with blossoms and leaves in accordance with her previous design, but as she could not carry out her ideas in this small space, a larger cardboard, 22 by 21 inches in size, was given her.

In carrying out her work on a larger scale [fig. 6] she again met great difficulties. After she had completed the outline of the pond, she started to place the trees. Each time, she finished one tree perfectly but never calculated space for the next one. This lack of visualization of the whole placed her once more in a desperate situation. She had to do the work over several times. The nearer she came to a certain "perfection," the stronger became her desire for further progress. She proceeded, under constant admonition to work slowly. In drawing the contents of the pond she easily found her way. She divided the whole pond with blue wavy lines, representing waves, and between them she placed fish, alternately blue and red. It is interesting to note that the alternating color rhythm found in the blossoms and leaves previously drawn is applied in the pictorial realization of her fish. Again the same principle occurs: a visual cognition reached by the creation of a previous configuration of form is applied in the formation of another, similar, structural order.

The accomplishment of the larger color drawing substantiates the fact that Selma is well able to extend her modest creative ability to a certain degree. It

Fig. 6. Pond with fish, bordered by trees. Selma's first large drawing (22 by 21 inches), done with colored crayons.

is presupposed, of course, that the selection of her subject matter lies in the realm of her interest, and further, that the pictorial execution takes place in full conformity with her stage of development of visual conception.

At about that same time, Selma was given the opportunity to make a design for a tablecloth twenty by thirty inches in size:

Working almost without interruption, she completed her design in one school day of six hours. The following week the drawing was transferred to linen, and Selma started to embroider, which she knew how to do in a simple way. She selected the color of the thread herself. This work [fig. 7] occupied her for several weeks, and during this time she became so absorbed in her task that nothing could disturb her. In the entire design, trees, flowers, and birds are clearly distinguished from one another; each figure is distinctly set

Fig. 7. Selma concentrated all her efforts for weeks on this tablecloth (20 by 30 inches), designed and embroidered by herself.

off from its surrounding ground, but all are vertically directed to a horizontal base line determined by the four borders. All parts of this design together constitute a unified organization of form in which no part can be changed without changing the other parts. It may seem obvious that an activity such as this requires the utmost application of self. For a full and just evaluation of her work, it must be noted that it has its origin in Selma's stage of visual conception and that it has been accomplished without any outside help. Attention and concentration were the consequence of her intense interest in her work. The same attitude was evident in her production of two hooked rugs which she also designed and executed [figs. 8 and 9].

In his concluding remarks about Selma, Schaefer-Simmern states:

Selma's major sphere of interest became more and more centered in her work. By choosing her colors, her enjoying the harmony of color-and-line combination and, finally, the organized pictures as a visually comprehensible totality, her emotional life became more overtly expressed than ever before. By constant control of the interrelationship of all pictorial elements and their mutually dependent effects her visual thinking was developed. By deciding upon her themes and materials as well as independently correcting distorted unity of form she evolved directed conceptual thinking. Finally, her work

Fig. 8 (above) and 9 (below). Selma's two hooked rugs, designed and executed by herself. (Each, 25 by 32 inches.)

caused a definite reorganization of her physical behavior. The tension of the particular arm muscle she used in her work affected the attitude of her entire body, as was seen most clearly when she assumed a complicated stance or position in the execution of a decisive line. All these factors operated in a constant interfunctional unity. They lose their significance as soon as they are separated from one another. They can only be understood and evaluated in their relation to the unified creative process and its effect upon the whole personality.

Figures 10–17 are works of other Southbury residents.

I was a frequent visitor to Schaefer-Simmern's studio, especially in the first year of his weekly, two-to-three-day stays at Southbury. The frequency of my visits in those early months was a consequence of what he showed me the second time we met. He came with a large portfolio containing artwork by "normal" individuals with whom he had worked in America and Germany. To say that I was surprised is to indulge in understatement. To say that I did not believe Schaefer-Simmern's explanation of their developments—that they were *their* creations, unin-

Fig. 10. "Pool surrounded by blossoming trees" (13 by 14 inches), by a woman of thirty-four with an IQ of 67, after nine months in the course.

Fig. 11. "Garden with bushes" (14 by 14 inches), by a woman of twenty-six with an IQ of 50, after eleven months in the course.

fluenced in content, composition, and direction by Schaefer-Simmern— is not an overstatement. Schaefer-Simmern *must* have played a very directive role. I had to see for myself.

No visitor to Schaefer-Simmern's studio at Southbury could fail to be dramatically impressed by the energy, interest, and persistence of the residents as they worked for several hours on their productions. Whatever stereotypes one had about the capacity of mentally retarded individuals to "concentrate" over long periods would be disconfirmed. Indeed, if you did not know that these adults were mentally retarded, you would say they were "ordinary" people engaged in an activity of vital concern to them. I am reminded here of a late friend who was a world-renowned radiologist. The first thing he would do with each new cadre of residents was to show them several X rays, ask them to study them, and then to write down what they saw. Unfailingly, the residents described a litany of pathology. But these were X rays of normal people.

Fig. 12. "Roosters between flowers and grass," an embroidery (13 by 14 inches) designed and executed by a young woman of thirty with an IQ of 76.

Fig. 13. Appliqué (14 by 14 inches) done by the same young woman.

Fig. 14. "Trees in blossom," design for a rug (40 by 30 inches) done in colored crayons by four mentally defective young women aged twenty, twenty-nine, thirty, and thirty-four. The upper two levels were done first and then repeated in reverse order. For the purpose of attaining an easy balance for the whole design, each level was started from the central tree and extended outward.

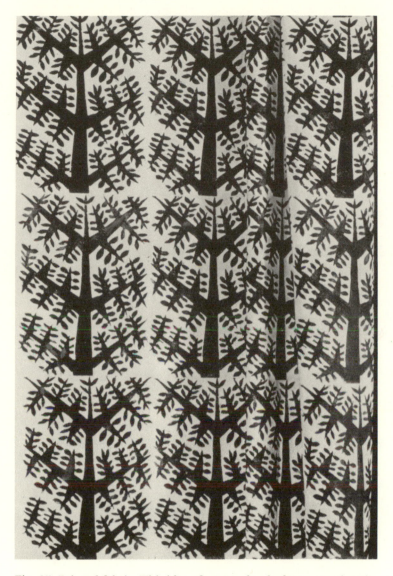

Fig. 15. Printed fabric. This idea of a tree, clearly demonstrating the stage of variability of direction of lines, was designed, cut in linoleum, and printed on cloth by a young woman of thirty with an IQ of 76. The work shows how early stages of artistic activity have that intrinsic decorative quality which is indispensable for a genuine applied work of art.

Fig. 16. "Paradise," colored drawing (40 by 30 inches) done as a cooperative work by five mentally defective boys and young men ranging in age from twelve to thirty years. A suggestion was given them of starting the entire design with the main theme "Adam and Eve under the Tree." The boys selected the center of the working area (four pieces of cardboard joined in one) as the right place for this theme; and thus they established the clearest figure-ground relationship. The other objects were pictorially organized by following a simple order of parallelism in relation to the central design and to each other.

Fig. 17. "Flower garden," a drawing made with oil crayons on a cotton sheet (40 by 30 inches), later pressed with a hot iron; a cooperative work done by five feebleminded boys aged eleven, twelve, thirteen, and fourteen years. Before drawing the flowers on cloth, each boy prepared his own flower thoroughly on a sheet of paper. Each level was started from the central design and extended outward.

To Schaefer-Simmern, his students were normal people in the sense that they had the capacity to create artistic forms. They were not devoid of creativity. His mind was not cluttered by a conception of intelligence that emphasize the capacity to form concepts, to abstract, to solve cognitive problems, to "think." For Schaefer-Simmern, artistic activity was quintessentially a problem-solving process in which what he termed "visual conceiving" was an omnipresent feature, a cognitive process that truly engaged the whole organism. But it was problem solving of a kind not contained in our customary conception of intelligence or tapped by intelligence tests. That the Southbury residents with whom he worked put their all into their artistic efforts, that they willingly struggled with the problems they encountered, that they strove to do it "better"—none of this was surprising to Schaefer-Simmern. It flabbergasted everyone who visited the studio.

Schaefer-Simmern never taught the group qua group. Each resident was aware of what others were doing. They would observe and seemingly study each other's work, occasionally they would talk to each other about their work, but in terms of content and composition, each resident went his or her own way. There were times, as the legends of several pictures indicate, when groups of residents worked cooperatively on a theme (such as "Paradise") suggested by Schaefer-Simmern. Each resident contributed in terms of what he or she had been working on. Schaefer-Simmern was, of course, crucial in showing them what was involved in going from a drawing to printed cloth, cotton sheet, or rug.

It was wondrous to behold what a beehive of learning and creativity that studio was. In contrast, Southbury's "industrial arts" building was like a factory assembly line, a contrast that engendered a good deal of hostility in those who directed that program.

Before coming to Southbury, Schaefer-Simmern had worked with residents in a New York reformatory. Their ages ranged from seventeen to twenty-two and their IQs from 72 to 107. A typical resident was Michael:

> Michael was twenty years of age, a first-generation American of Greek descent, in religion a Catholic. He had a very limited educational background, having attended school only to the third grade because of illness. In a state school which he attended for a short time he gained some knowledge of carpentry. After this he helped his mother, who worked as a superintendent of two buildings in New York City. The psychological report describes him as "an immature youth who had developed deep feelings of inferiority due largely to little mingling with people and poor educational background. He

is lacking in confidence, both in himself and socially. . . . He is quite unable to handle himself among more aggressive boys. . . . He is very passive and timid. . . . His intelligence quotient is 76, which places him near the borderline of mental defective."

Michael at first appeared quiet and reserved. He seemed depressed, but was friendly. He did not display interest and seemed rather indifferent to the work. At the suggestion that he draw whatever he liked, he made a clumsy animal that could have been done by a child of about eight years of age [fig. 18]. Asked what his drawing represented, he replied: "A horse. I always like to be near horses. When I see one, I walk up to it and pet it. I have a natural feeling for horses just like I have for dogs." Referring to his picture, he said: "But I don't like it. It's no good." Michael was not asked why he did not like his drawing, for then he would have had to explain it in verbal terms, that is, abstractly. Since this might have hindered him from judging his pictures visually, he was simply given the suggestion of drawing, in accordance with his own ideas, a "better horse." The term "better" did not influence him, for it left him free to apply it as he wished.

Figure 19 is a product of four weeks of work:

Michael's interest in his work was best expressed when he entered the workshop a week later. "All this week I have thought about my horse. I know what I'm going to do." Surprisingly, he selected a much larger sheet of paper (30 by 40 inches) and started to draw a new picture of a horse. Since he had difficul-

Fig. 18. Michael's first drawing.

Fig. 19. After four weeks of participation in the course, Michael reached the stage at which he realized for the first time the overlapping of limbs.

ties in handling this sheet of paper on the workbench, he decided to build an easel. The enlargement of his drawing presented difficulties, but he did not give up and displayed a perseverance he had never shown before. He had to draw his theme over and over again. After having done five pictures which were not to his satisfaction, he finally succeeded [fig. 20]. He observed his drawing for a long time, as he was constantly advised to do, and then decided to fill in the entire picture with brown color in order to make a brown horse. In order to distinguish the legs from the body, he drew the overlappings in white. The drawing represents a horse, its right foreleg lifted, standing on a ground with grass and a bush in front of it.

The first impression of this drawing is an impression of much greater tension throughout the entire figure. The tension can only be attributed to the fact that Michael applied his stage of visual conception—that is, the relationship of variability of direction—to the entire figure in a much higher degree than in his earlier pictures. Even the movement in the right front leg can only be explained by this fact. But note the changes in the legs nearest the observer in relation to the body. Their outlines, which still carry figural meanings against the body, which represents ground meaning, are no longer closed. They are open at the top. This means a further application of the stage of borderless transition, the figural meaning of the outlined areas of these legs going over, borderless, into areas of the body which carry ground

Fig. 20. By means of greater application of the principle of variability of lines, more tension in the entire figure of the horse was attained.

meaning. The horse is now visually conceived as a new, coherent, intentional figure on the more differentiated stage of visual conceiving.

The fact that this comparatively complicated pictorial configuration is attained by Michael's spontaneous ability to conceive visually new relationships of form, so that one form emerges out of the preceding one, points clearly to the organic development of his creative abilities.

The discovery that he was able to perform unexpected tasks gave Michael new courage. He saw other boys of the same experimental group cutting their designs in linoleum and printing them on cloth for window curtains to be used in a new building at the institution. He felt that he could do the same thing, using his design of a horse, bush, and grass. The size of the curtain was measured, to determine whether the design of a single horse with bush and grass could be repeated crosswise. Michael considered the problem a moment, and said: "Why not use trees and bushes? I know how to make a tree." But when he tried his design on paper the size of the window curtain, using the rhythm of large tree, horse with bush, large tree, bush and horse, large tree, he decided to let the two horses face the center tree [fig. 21]. When he came to the design of the large tree, he drew his previous differentiated form

Fig. 21. Michael's design to be used for a window curtain.

(right-hand side of picture) on a piece of linoleum. His difficulties began when he started to cut it out; piece after piece broke off, and soon the design could not be used at all. "I have to make a simpler tree," he concluded, and in using a simpler configuration of form he came to the present design. When he drew the horse, he added a mane in a plain way but nevertheless followed a definite structural order. He drew a new shape for the horse's tail. Within the outline of the tail he drew the lines for the hair in a relationship of direction to the outline. In the formation of the mane he applied the same principle.

The process of cutting out the figures in linoleum took him a long time, especially since it required careful work for the small details. He obviously had difficulty because his big, clumsy hands were not used to such delicate work. But he never asked for help, and proceeded slowly for two days. The printing was done in a simple manner. After the two blocks of linoleum were covered with oil colors blended with permanent mixture, the material was printed by hammering the blocks on it. Each block had to be fitted exactly to the neighboring one. In making the first two lines, Michael needed help, but the rest he was able to do by himself. When he finished the last line, he expressed his satisfaction: "Gee, that's lots of fun. I should make one for my mother at home." And turning to the writer, he said: "When you go to New York tomorrow, will you go to my mother and ask her if she wants a curtain and find out how big she wants it? I want to make her one."

After he had completed the window curtain, all his drawings were shown to him in the sequence of their production. He was obviously astonished, and could hardly believe that he had done them. This fact evidently must have impressed him. He, who was always sparing with words and had never spoken of his home, felt impelled to reveal a new aspect of his personality to his mother. Perhaps he wanted to make good at something, because he repeated his wish again, with the supplementary remark: "You see, when I write my mother it takes a couple of days till she gets my letter and it's hard for her to write. She's got lots to do." Self-respect, gained through productive work, created either a new or at least an increased relationship to his home, especially to his mother. He obviously felt a new worth within him which apparently he wanted to reveal to her.

Figure 22 was Michael's last work.

A final example is Miss E, a social worker.[3] Figure 23 is her first

---

3. Schaefer's book has long, picture-filled chapters titled: "The Experiment: Defectives"; "The Experiment: Delinquents"; "The Experiment: Refugees"; "The Experiment with Persons in Business and the Professions." For obvious reasons, I am only able to present samples suggestive of the development of the persons with whom he worked. If what I have written and shown stimulates readers to read and *look* at the book's contents, I will have accomplished one of my major goals.

Figure 22. After seven months of participation in the course, Michael achieved this, his last work, a relief (11 by 20 inches) modeled in clay and cast in artificial stone.

Fig. 23. Miss E's first drawings.

drawing. One of her last, used as the frontispiece and on the dust cover of Schaefer-Simmern's book, is reproduced as figure 24, and in color on the dust jacket of this book.

Observing Schaefer-Simmern with the residents was both instructive and mystifying. When a resident showed him his or her work, Schaefer-Simmern *studied* it for several minutes. What was there about the work

Fig. 24. "Negro Boy Sitting in Morningside Park," done by a thirty-seven-year-old social worker.

that required such serious thought? It took me several weeks and countless long discussions with him to understand that he was examining the work in terms of forms and their interrelationships—how one aspect (line or color or both) determined and was determined by adjoining aspects, their unity, their figure-ground relationships. It never would occur to him to respond in terms of "I like it" or "I don't like it." More often than not, he would react by asking, "Do *you* like it? Can you do it *better?*" I never heard a resident say that he or she could not do it better, regardless of whether he or she liked or disliked the work. Occasionally, Schaefer-Simmern would say, sympathetically: "You had trouble with this, didn't you?" Later, Schaefer-Simmern would tell me, *show* me, which aspect of the work was not in conformity with other aspects in terms of direction of line, or overlapping of lines, thus in some way interfering with a good visual gestalt. It was, of course, very difficult for the residents to put into language what the difficulty had been. But they could point to parts of the picture that had troubled them. Schaefer-Simmern might then suggest that they use a large sheet of paper or try different colors. No less frequently he would say: "Study this. Take your time. Then try it again and try to do it better so you see it the way you want to see it." I was constantly amazed at the way in which Schaefer-Simmern's manner conveyed his respect for the residents as people and artists.

Especially when residents were experiencing difficulty of some kind, Schaefer-Simmern would serially spread out for them their own development. He would point out when they had had difficulty, why they had it, and how they had overcome it. Observing those interactions was quite revelatory and amazing because here were two people, as different from each other as two humans can be, one mentally retarded and the other an intellectual, seriously discussing problems in the creation of works of art.

Schaefer-Simmern was possessed by one belief and one "theory." The belief was that artistic activity was a universal human attribute. The theory was that artistic activity developed in stages, each of which had a governing cognitive principle of visual conception, beginning with scribbles and circular forms and proceeding to stages requiring the use of perspective. The process by which an individual creates visual forms in accord with his or her stage of development is also the process by which the individual gets formed in some respect. It occasioned no surprise in Schaefer-Simmern that this process and development altered people's conception of themselves and how they looked at their world.

In his *Talks to Teachers on Psychology*, William James said: "I say that you make a great, a very great mistake, if you think that psychology, being the science of the mind's laws, as something from which you can deduce definite programs and schemes and methods of instruction for immediate schoolroom use. Psychology is a science, and teaching an art, and sciences never generate arts directly out of themselves. An intermediary inventive mind must make the application, by using its originality" (pp. 7–8).Schaefer-Simmern had a quintessentially inventive mind, an inventiveness tied to a capacity to empathize with or grasp the specific problem with which the artist was grappling. That grasp, of course, was based indirectly on his conception of developmental stages, but that conception did not tell him when, why, or how to respond to the artist and the artistic problem. Nor did it emphasize in any formal way the truly basic importance of *respect* for what the person was trying to do, however simple. Schaefer-Simmern was utterly incapable of suffering fools gladly, and to him the earth was populated largely by fools. But faced with anyone seriously confronting the creation of artistic form, Schaefer-Simmern accorded boundless interest and respect, regardless of any other personal judgment he might make about that person.

If it is appropriate to label Schaefer-Simmern as artist, art theorist, and educator, it is also incomplete. He was a social philosopher in that he saw his work in terms of how, in our society, the creative capacities of people either are not recognized or are extinguished, thus impoverishing and constricting their development and lives. Not only are their own creative capacities not recognized and nurtured, but they are also rendered incapable of recognizing and nurturing the artistic activity of others. It was not for Schaefer-Simmern himself that he did what he did with the Southbury residents. Indeed, he did not come to Southbury to "prove" what he had already demonstrated with diverse "ordinary" people. He came as a way of showing the world how vastly underestimated was the universality of artistic creativity. If the world said that these residents were devoid of creativity, he would show otherwise. So Schaefer-Simmern arranged for an exhibition of Selma's work in her cottage, which for one weekend became an art gallery, to which people came in droves. It was his hope, quite unrealistic, that when people saw what Selma (and others) had done they would alter existing programs, they would start taking seriously the implications of what they saw for existing training and educational programs that produced drones. For Schaefer-Simmern, artistic activity was not only a way of creating a work of art on paper or other materials but a way of seeing, transforming, acting on one's surround. Artistic activity was a mode of thinking, experiencing, and doing what our traditional conceptions of intelligence ignored and relegated to the category of "special" because of the importance attached to abstract learning by regnant societal values.

I end this chapter with a personal anecdote that may be as helpful to the reader as the experience was to me. Schaefer-Simmern took me to the Metropolitan Museum of Art in New York and stood me before a painting by Poussin of a farm scene. I told him that Brooklyn-Manhattan-Newark me did not like farm scenes. To which Schaefer-Simmern replied: "Your task now is not to determine whether you like a painting or not. Study the painting by asking what you can change in any part of the painting, color or form, without then having to change anything else in the surround. Take your time and study the painting." It did not take me long to realize that if I changed this or that in this or that way I would have to change other aspects of the surround—indeed, the entire painting. For the first time I truly understood what Schaefer-Simmern meant by a configurated whole in which figure-ground relationships could not be changed without introducing a jarring note into one's perception of the painting. I did not end up "liking" the painting, but I surely appreciated as never before what an artist confronts in organizing color and form consistent with his or her visual conception. And Schaefer-Simmern ended the conversation by saying: "There is a world of difference between a Poussin and a Selma, but there is also an identity in that both struggled in a process that required not only a clear internal visual conception but an ordering of color and form that satisfied what they wanted to see, what they had to see. Poussin and Selma had no intention of copying nature but of realizing that internal visual conception, their reality".

4 ◆ THE SUBSTANCE
OF THE CHALLENGE

Wherein lies the challenge of artistic activity to psychology? If we assume that creativity is a universal human attribute, what would it mean if we took that seriously? One part of the answer is that we would examine and reevaluate the emphasis placed on the development of logical-scientific thinking as a preeminent goal informing the socialization and education of children. That does not mean, of course, a devaluation of such a goal, but rather accepting that there are other modes of thinking and producing which, if not nurtured, dilute the capacity to use, master, and enjoy certain ways of transacting with one's world. I am reminded here of B. F. Skinner's *Walden Two* because, if anything is clear in that book, it is Skinner's recognition of the crucial significance of artistic activity in living. In his preface to the 1976 edition he says:

> Although sometimes questioned, the survival value of art, music, literature, games and other activities not tied to the serious business of life is clear enough. A culture must positively reinforce the behavior of those who support it and must avoid creating negative reinforcers from which its members will escape through defection. A world which has been made beautiful and exciting by artists, composers, writers, and performers, is as important for survival as one which satisfies biological needs. (P. xiii)

No one would accuse Skinner of seeking to devalue the acquiring of logical-scientific modes of thinking and investigating, but what has gone relatively unnoticed by his readers and critics is the coequal value he places on artistic activity from a developmental and social standpoint. If Skinner's formal psychology can be criticized on various grounds, he cannot be faulted for pointing out the discrepancy between what people are and what they can be. Indeed, it would be understandable if the reader concluded from his book that the stifling of creativity, especially in the arts, is very high on Skinner's list of evils.

To my knowledge, in the vast corpus of his writings, it is only in *Walden Two* that he emphasizes the "survival value" of artistic activity. Like all other psychological theorists, he has little or nothing to say about the recognition and nurturing of artistic activity in the course of development, whether in real life or in his utopia, Walden Two. In applying his principles to problems in living, Skinner and his followers have given no attention to creativity in its diverse manifestations. For example, Skinnerian principles have been extensively employed with mentally retarded individuals, but in none of these instances does one sense that these individuals are regarded as other than devoid of the capacity to create. Quite a contrast to Schaefer-Simmern, who truly took seriously not only that artistic activity was a human attribute but also that the ways in which it was extinguished contributed to an impoverished existence.

A second aspect of the challenge derives from the observation, made by numerous writers, that the creativity of children is lost as they get older. For example, Jean Piaget, who devoted his life to trying to understand how we acquire logical-scientific ways of thinking about and dealing with the world, states:

> Two paradoxical facts surprise all who are accustomed to study the development of the mental functions and aptitudes of the child. The first is that very often the young child appears more gifted than the older child in the fields of drawing, of symbolic expression such as plastic representation, participation in spontaneously organized collective activities, and so on, and sometimes in the domain of music. If we study the intellectual functions or the social sentiments of the child, development appears to be more or less a continuous progression, whereas in the realm of artistic expression, on the contrary, the impression gained is frequently one of retrogression. . . . The second of these facts, which in part can be equated with the first, is that it is much more difficult to establish regular stages of development in the case of artistic tendencies than it is in that of other mental functions. . . . Without an appropriate art education which will succeed in cultivating these means of expression and in encouraging these first manifestations of aesthetic creation, the actions of adults and the restraints of school and family life have the effect in most cases of checking or thwarting such tendencies instead of enriching them. (Gardner, 1973, p. 18)

After an extensive review of the literature on the arts and human development, Gardner says: "Certainly the average adult is notoriously lacking in sensitivity—the artistically naive adult and the average 10-year-old perform about the same on aesthetic appreciation tests. Yet, while it might prove difficult to train the typical adult, whose tastes are formed, there are greater hopes of sharpening the artistic capacity of the growing child. We have suggested some approaches in the above discussion" (p. 295).

It is puzzling that what Piaget terms a "retrogression" and Gardner an "atrophying" has not stimulated the curiosity of psychologists. Gardner is surely right when he says that "far more extensive examination will be required" before we understand better the atrophying of artistic activity. But he does not ask why that examination has not taken place and probably will not take place. It is also puzzling that Gardner, who refers briefly to Schaefer-Simmern's work, does not note, let alone emphasize, that this issue is central to Schaefer's book, and that he has presented compelling evidence that the atrophying is not a peculiarity of individuals but a consequence of cultural-educational conceptions of what is art and non-art and who is and is not creative. In short, the atrophying is testimony to the strength of factors that deny that artistic activity is a universal attribute, thus making it virtually impossible to regard such activity as something other than special and, therefore, not to be accorded the importance given to the development of logical-scientific modes of thinking. It is akin to the dynamics of the wish-fulfilling prophecy: you start with a conception that initiates actions that "validate" the initial conception, unaware that if you began with the opposite conception the consequences might be discernibly different. It is also kin to the dynamics of "blaming the victim": explaining the atrophying by deficits *in* the individual.

Because Schaefer-Simmern was one of the few who seriously believed that creativity was a universal human attribute, he had to look at the educational process: its goals, methods, practices. How, if at all, did that process recognize and nurture creativity in general and artistic activity in particular? How did it recognize and build on the concrete experience and developmental levels of children? To what extent did that process require children to acquire concepts and abstractions that did not emerge from their concrete sensory experience and to conform to external criteria of meaning that had little relationship to their phenomenology: their modes, level, and content of experience?

There were few things to which Schaefer-Simmern was affectively neutral. And nothing aroused more anger and despair in him than his observations of what went on in the classrooms of our schools. Schaefer-Simmern was no bleeding-heart liberal, and he was incapable of waxing sentimental about the innocence of children and the tender care they required. He could become livid at those who espoused what he termed the "cult of expressiveness," the view that it was vitally important for a child to express him- or herself almost regardless of the form of that expression and the developmental uses it served. To Schaefer-Simmern, *dis*ordered expressiveness was no less an abomination than the mindless repetition of cognitively undigested "memory games" so characteristic of children in classrooms. Unlike Piaget and Gardner, Schaefer-Simmern could not talk or think of the development of artistic activity only in terms of Western societies. His magnum opus, which he never brought to completion but the "visual data" for which I have seen, came from scores of societies: in the present, the near and far past, so-called primitive and otherwise. As he would frequently say, retrogression and atrophying are not features of the many societies in which over the course of a lifetime the members engage in some form of artistic activity. They may not regard what they do as art, they frequently do not have the conception of "art," we may not "like" what they make, but they nevertheless produce works of art distinguished by their organization of form, color, and materials.

It was not until the latter half of the nineteenth century that Western artists became appreciative of and influenced by so-called primitive art. And it was not until the present century that the ethnographies of anthropologists made it clear that artistic activity was part and parcel of the daily activities of the people in these cultures—baskets, rugs, pottery, and icons of diverse kinds. It goes without saying that in these cultures people differ in the quality and complexity of their artistic efforts, but the significant point is that one would be hard put to conclude from the anthropological evidence that retrogression and atrophying occur in primitive cultures as they do in our society. If that is the case, then their occurrence in our society is a matter of great importance, theoretically and practically. At the very least, it justifies asking this question: is it possible that our conception of human abilities is so biased and in-complete, so suffused with certain values and expectations, that we underestimate what people are capable of? Is this not another example of how we like to believe that we have so liberated ourselves from the suffocating traditions and worldviews of past centuries that we have no comparable blind spots today? Are we exempt from the lesson of human history that worldviews are not self-correcting, that each era has its blind spots, that worldviews change only after the axioms which sustain them are challenged and then demonstrated to be invalid?

Let me now pose the challenge in terms of another universal human attribute far more familiar to most readers than artistic activity, albeit inextricably related to it. I refer to the fact that question asking is a feature of all people, of all ages, of all times. We are used to hearing that man is a question-asking organism. This is not a special characteristic that some people have and others do not. And we are used to hearing from parents the ambivalence engendered in them by the constant flood of questions their children put to them. On the one hand, they regard such behavior positively because it bespeaks a curiosity about self and the world indicative of intelligence and brightness; on the other hand, they are frequently nonplused as to how to answer many of the questions in ways appropriate to the child's developmental level. No theorist of human development downplays the significance of question asking, and none would argue that to stifle question asking has favorable consequences. On the contrary, to stifle question asking in a child is far more likely than not to have adverse consequences for that child's development. Question asking should be taken and responded to seriously. And if the rate of your child's question asking requires for computation a hand calculator, that is a better state of affairs than if the frequency is small! Better too many than too few!

What happens to the rate of question asking when a child begins school? I have spent countless hours in classrooms. None of my observations stemmed from an interest in question asking. It took me a while to become aware of the obvious: the classroom was not a place where children asked questions. They answered, they did not ask questions.

Given the importance attached to question asking for cognitive development, one would expect it to be the object of extensive study in education. The fact is that there have been fewer than a score of such studies in this century! The most recent, and certainly the most sophisticated, was carried out by Edwin Susskind in 1969. He notes with surprise not only that the relevant literature is scanty but that previous studies come to similar conclusions. Susskind developed procedures for noting and categorizing questions asked by children and teachers in social studies periods in a suburban school. These were forty- to forty-five-minute periods. Before doing the study he asked teachers and administrators to estimate the number of questions children and teachers would ask in these periods. *Susskind found that the average number of questions asked by children was approximately two (and those might have been asked by one child). The average number of questions asked by teachers ranged from 40 to over 150.* Needless to say, the estimates by teachers and administrators were way off the mark. On the countless occasions I have presented Susskind's study to educators and others, no one has ever said that the findings were "good" in the sense that they reflected what a classroom *should* be. Far from trying to justify the findings as supportive of good practice, everyone expressed chagrin, disappointment, and bewilderment. As one teacher asked: "How do you explain the fact that although everybody agrees that question asking is necessary for learning, our practice says that we are not taking it seriously?"

There are several reasons I have introduced question asking in a discussion of artistic activity. The first is that, unlike artistic activity, question asking is viewed as a universal human attribute, and yet, despite this agreement, it is not taken seriously in a learning-developmental context as crucial as schooling itself. It is beyond the scope of this book to try to explain this grotesque discrepancy. I have discussed this in some detail in my book *Schooling in America: Scapegoat and Salvation* (1983). What needs to be said here is that if question asking were taken seriously, it would require dramatic changes in how classrooms and schools are organized and how educational personnel are selected and educated. It is not simply a matter of resolve or even greater clarity about the significance of question asking for productive exploration and learning, although they are crucial first steps. It is, by analogy, like a work of art: changing one aspect has consequences for other aspects.

If the studies on question asking have had absolutely no effect on educational practice, this is in part (and only in part) because of their implications for how people and contexts will have to change. Similarly, if one comes to the conclusion that creativity and artistic activity are universal human attributes, the implications of that conclusion for parental and educational practices are no less consequential. It is far less consequential if one adheres to the view that artistic activity, unlike question asking, is a "special" attribute. It is this view that explains, again only in part, why art education is so frequently absent from the curriculum or is seen as an add-on luxury or assigned a certain number of minutes on a couple of days for drawing or coloring or making something the teacher has assigned. The studies on question asking demonstrate how imprisoned teachers are—by virtue of their training and not their personal characteristics—by the belief that their major goal is to pour facts and information into students, at the expense of the questions children have. What passes for art education in our schools is no less determined by the belief that the child should conform to someone else's reality and interests. Is it any wonder that creativity is about the last word that would enter one's mind after observing the modal classroom, be it in a school in an affluent or a nonaffluent neighborhood?

Another reason for bringing in question asking is that it is a ubiquitous feature of the artistic process, albeit one that has hardly been noted or studied. Precisely because it is a process that requires the choice and use of materials to produce a configuration appropriate to an internal visual conception, it engenders problems, and therefore questions, about how to achieve the sought-for configuration. It is quite the opposite of "copying" that conception. You start with the conception; you begin to organize it "out there"; you quickly find that there are problems in composition, line, color, and size; the internal conception undergoes change; you reorganize aspects of what you have done; and the process continues until you are satisfied or give up in frustration. And throughout the process you are asking questions of yourself and of the changing product. No one denies that the artistic process has all the features of problem solving—what some have termed "visual thinking" because it has a logic peculiar to the organization of visual forms. It is problem solving that at every step is marked by question asking. I have observed countless preschoolers engaging in some form of artistic activity, and I have been struck by their facial expressions indicative of question asking. I was no less struck by the failure of adults to be sensitive to and to respond helpfully to what was puzzling to the child. What happens so frequently—and this is most glaring when the child is in school—is that adults will show the child what to do (that is, how to copy reality), unaware that they are not taking account of the substantive questions and developmental level of the child. As Susskind's study of question asking in the classroom demonstrates, it is as if the questions of children are either nonexistent or interfering or a distraction to be ignored.

Creativity is not a characteristic in and of *an* individual. At the very least, it requires a context that contains materials and opportunities that can be used for artistic purposes. These exist in some form and degree in every culture, regardless of the type and site. In this sense one could say that every individual engages in artistic activity. But cultures differ dramatically in at least three respects. The first is the opportunities they provide to *observe* artistic activity—for example, making baskets, clothing, pottery, and kindred artifacts. The second is the opportunity the culture provides to *engage in* artistic activity. And the third is the *support* it provides for such engagement. The support may be formal or informal, but its distinguishing characteristic is that it *anticipates* and *reinforces* such activity. A colleague of mine put it this way: "During the scores of decades that the Chartres Cathedral was being built, people of *all* ages observed the work of diverse artisans, they participated in the building, they were expected to do so, and that engagement was central to their worldview. They were surrounded by and participated in works of art, although our concept of art was not theirs." Modern society provides far fewer opportunities to observe and engage in artistic activity. And those consequences of "progress" have been accompanied by a view of human potential that relegates artistic activity to the status of a special ability, an activity crucial to neither individual nor societal development.

If the frequency of question asking by children in classrooms is so low, this does not mean, of course, that they are not inwardly asking questions about themselves and their world. It does mean that while they remain question-asking organisms, they are learning that asking questions is not an especially rewarded behavior. As anyone who has worked psycho-therapeutically with children can attest, getting children to give voice to their questions is not an easy matter. That is true, albeit less so, with children not requiring personal help. If humans are question-asking organisms, if question asking is viewed by every developmental theorist as something to be treasured, supported, and productively channeled, we are far from taking it seriously. Between theory and practice is a minefield of societal values and institutional forms and goals that have made for a gulf that seems unbridgeable.

It has been noted that near the end of secondary schooling there appears to be a return of interest in diverse artistic activities: visual, musical, literary, crafts, dance. Gardner concludes:

> This developmental picture has led some scholars to speak of a U-shaped curve in artistic development. The first part of the U refers to the apparently high level of creativity found among preschoolers; the trough of the U desig-nates the period of literalness, when the child's artistic creations are less striking in the eyes of many observers; the triumphant resurgence of the U marks the attainment (on the part of at least some adolescents) of a new, higher level of artistic accomplishment. Debate has focused on whether each end of the U designates the same kind of competence or whether, instead, the kind of creativity exhibited by most preschoolers is of a fundamentally differ-ent order from that found in the minority of adolescents who are artistically accomplished. (P. 88)

The U-shaped curve in artistic development is valid as description, but its significances have to be seen in relation to the fact that there are cultures in which that curve is either nonexistent or minimally so. It also has to be seen in relation to observations of some private schools in our society, where artistic activity is coequal in value (and time) with other subject matter. I have observed schools in the Rudolf Steiner tradition where arts and crafts are central to learning anything; that is, they not only promote artistic development in a narrow sense but also demonstrate how the arts can be related to traditional subject matter. The U-shaped curve says less about artistic development than it does about worldviews and their educational consequences in our society.[1]

In regard to the renewed interest in creative activity that some adolescents display, one consideration deserves emphasis. In mentioning it here I have no intention of oversimplifying an explanation of the U-shaped curve, but it is a consideration that tends to be glossed over. I refer to the need and desire of the growing child literally to put his or her personal stamp on some aspect of the surround. It is part of the process of forming a personal identity, but it is more than an internal, private affair in that the child seeks to see that identity reflected in some way "out there," to "show" others a reflection of his or her uniqueness. This can be manifested in countless and seemingly (to others) insignificant ways—for example, the clothes one likes to wear, how one likes food organized on a plate, how one's possessions or one's room are organized, the artifacts one makes or collects, the content and style of telling story-fantasies to friends and others. It is a process in which the developing sense of identity is given overt and ordered expression. At the same time that the child may seek to be like others, that same child feels apart and seeks to give expression to that sense of uniqueness. And that need to express—in the original Latin sense "to press out"—is never extinguished. It may be blunted, inhibited, or even punished, but it cannot be extinguished. What Gardner rightly characterizes as "the apparently high level of creativity found among preschoolers" says less about the sensitivity of adults to the creativity of preschoolers than it does about the developmental unimportance most adults assign to the preschooler's play. If that creativity, that need to give some kind of

---

1. Richardson's *In the Early World* (1964) contains one of the most inspiring and instructive accounts of a school in which arts and crafts were the media through which artistic expression and scientific exploration took place. Richardson, a scientist and untrained teacher, started with a one-room public school in New Zealand, and with his young students created an educational community that would have warmed the hearts of Schaefer-Simmern, John Dewey, and Kenneth Koch. What took place in that school was completely unpredictable by the U-curve hypothesis. Fortunately, Richards knew nothing about the hypothesis, but he knew a great deal about how to capitalize on the interests and capabilities of developing children and their need to feel a sense of mastery of themselves and diverse media for ordered expression. It is a gem of a book.

external form to what one wants to express, receives little or no support in the course of formal schooling, this is no basis for concluding that the need is absent.

I am reminded here of those long-ago days when I was in elementary school. The Hawthorne Avenue School in Newark, New Jersey, had a "manual training shop." Beginning around the fifth grade every male student went to that shop twice a week. It was a large room that looked like an architect's studio: high, diagonally slanted desks, stools (not chairs), T-squares, metal triangles of varying sizes, large pieces of heavy paper, thumb tacks galore, and walls containing drawings and blue-prints. I never entered that shop without feeling that I was in an adult world, quite a contrast to the regular classroom. And I looked forward eagerly to the skills I would acquire and what I would *make. I* would be *making* something that would in some way be *mine,* a reflection of *me.*

However, it was a horrendous experience. I was told what to copy, how to use different instruments, when to use this or that kind of pencil or stylus, and, fatefully, why it was sinful to draw lines and angles that were other than neatly perfect so as to require another piece of precious paper. Whatever the reason—anxiety, clumsiness, sloppiness—I was in the teacher's opinion a lost cause. This was one of several experiences that convinced me I lacked whatever was required to translate via eye, hand, and media an internal visual conception in visible form. It also helps explain why, when I took geometry in high school, I barely passed the course. I still remember, with unfortunate vividness, when in the first week in that geometry course the teacher drew two connecting lines on the board and said it was an obtuse angle. Why call it an obtuse angle? What did the word *obtuse* mean? Where did it come from? For that matter, what did geometry mean? I was plagued by these and similar questions but never articulated one of them. As in manual training, my job was to learn what someone else thought was mean-ingful and important.

Question asking and the need to feel and be creative—to be able to put one's personal stamp on what one does—go underground during schooling, but they are not extinguished. The turmoil we associate with adolescence has, of course, many sources, but they all revolve about the forging of an identity that will be recognized and respected by others. It is a process in which a sense of independence and separateness is sought that will allow the individual to go his or her own way. If the process is marked by internal and external conflict, if for too many individuals the obstacles are overcome only in small measure, let us not overlook that the process seeks to create and express that identity. It should not be surprising, therefore, if the creativity so obvious in pre-schoolers reappears in some adolescents. Why, as Gardner notes, in a minority and not a majority of adolescents? This is not a question that has occupied psychologists. To conclude that artistic activity is a special talent is a premature, mischievous, and dangerous explanation because it confuses the way things are with the way they might be. Indeed, it completely and blithely ignores cultural attitudes toward artistic ac-tivity, educational practice, and contrary anthropological evidence. It is not unlike the old argument, which many psychologists supported and for which they provided "evidence," that because males and fe-males were biologically different, all observable developmental and behavioral and role-work differences between them reflect "biology as destiny."

What is at issue here is more than whether creative expression is a universal human attribute and how to account for individual dif-ferences. No less at issue is what it means for people to come to regard themselves, and to be regarded by others, as incapable of any form of artistic expression that puts their distinctive stamp on something. Most people carry this attitude with them throughout their lives. It is not an attitude with which they entered the world. Rather, it is an accommoda-tion to long-standing cultural views and educational practices.

There is no doubt that in this century Freud and Piaget have had the most pervasive impact on psychological understanding of children and adolescents. Although their writings were far from ignored, it was not until after World War II that they became household names in psychol-ogy and the society generally, and deservedly so. Why did recognition and acclaim come after World War II? In the case of psychoanalysis, the answer is quite complicated, involving the history and traditions of American medicine, the narrowness of American psychology, the em-phasis on biology in American psychiatry, the second-class status of psychiatry in American medicine, and the nature and force of the puritannical streak in American culture. I have discussed this at some length in *The Making of an American Psychologist*. One cannot understand the legitimation of psychoanalysis in the university and society without comprehending the upheavals in society during and after World War II. Those upheavals were cultural, intellectual, professional, and in-stitutional in their consequences. Succinctly put, American psychology and psychiatry were found wanting in numerous ways in their response to the war-produced upheavals; their theories and methods were inadequate to explain and cope with the problems of transformed personal and social living and the explicit public, governmental recognition that those problems had to be dealt with. Psychoanalysis held out the promise of explaining these problems and even helping to overcome them. In an amazingly short period, psychoanalysis, as theory, practice, and research orientation, attained a status never dreamed of by its proponents. Psychoanalysis was an encompassing theory of human development. But its most novel, compelling, and controversial aspect was how it described, explained, and illuminated the complex drama of childhood. And that drama spoke to concerns of post–World War II parents intent on rearing their children in ways quite different from their parents', more appropriate to the post–World War II world. If Dr. Spock's (1945) book on child rearing came to rival the Bible in sales, this reflected the perplexities of parents and their need for direction. And his book reflected Freud's influence.

We can read Freud and his epigones in one of two ways. One is that childhood is a minefield of interpersonal conflicts and obstacles from which no child escapes and which form the child in fateful ways. The dependency and vulnerabilities of the young child, embedded in and transacting with a familial context, make conflict inevitable. From its earliest days the child is no empty vessel. It has needs and drives, perceptual and cognitive capacities, that are always, so to speak, on a collision course with parental obligations to socialize the child. The collisions may be small or large in their consequence for the child's affective and cognitive development, but collisions are inevitable. The striving, purposeful child collides with a no less striving and purposeful surround.

Another way, not contradictory to the first, of reading Freud is that the child is a seeker constantly trying out ways of making an impact on someone or something. The child is a curious, question-asking experimenter seeking to make sense of something, as much an initiator as a responder. Children are creative in that they transform and give ordered expression to internal imagery of diverse kinds. It may not appear ordered to adults, but it is not random expression. To my knowledge, Freud said little or nothing about creativity in children, although it seems clear he viewed the play of children and the stories they make up as more than the fulfillment of wishes and affective needs, or a means of coping with conflict. Although Freud had a passionate interest in art, particularly visual art, he never discussed it in relation to creativity in children. He was far more interested in fathoming the substance and vicissitudes of drives and conflicts. So, for example, when he wrote on Da Vinci, it was an effort to relate early fantasies and conflicts to the content of a Da Vinci painting. The word and the concept of creativity occur infrequently in Freud's writings. Faced with explaining the artist, Freud said, psychoanalysis must lay down its arms.

It is no criticism of Freud to point out that he had little to say about creativity in general and in children in particular. But when one examines the vast corpus of writings that Freud spawned, it is noteworthy how little attention has been given to the manifestations of artistic activity in children, to explaining its relative or total disappearance during the school years and its reappearance in only a minority of individuals in later years. Freud intended his theory to be an encompassing one, illuminating the springs and course of human development. His goal was not modest. But, like those who followed him, he gave no serious attention to explaining how cultural attitudes, values, and practices inhibit and overwhelm engagement in artistic activity. Unlike Schaefer-Simmern, Freud did not start with the assumption that artistic activity is a universal human attribute and, therefore, he could not ask why *in our culture* that attribute takes the unfortunate course it does. One of Freud's greatest achievements was to take seriously the significance of a particular human attribute: dreaming. It would be more correct to say that his achievement inhered in illustrating how something as private as dreaming was intimately related, among other things, to events in daily life—how those events trigger and become part of the content of dreams. One cannot but be impressed with the Talmudic-like thoroughness with which he sought to relate external events and settings to the substance and process of dreaming. That kind of seriousness and thoroughness has not been applied to the manifestations of creativity. Any theory of psychological development that ignores or glosses over artistic activity—its nature, course, and cultural embeddedness—is neither encompassing not capable of deepening further our view of the human organism.

If World War II created the social drama that facilitated the legitimation of psychoanalysis, it did the same for Piaget, much of whose important work was done before the war. It is a simple and clearer story because his monumental work spoke to a worldview that was dramatically increased in strength and pervasiveness by the war. I refer to the view that science, which had contributed so much to the Allied victory in the war, would and should transform the world, that it was the basis for constructing a new world in which the ills and deficits of the old world would be overcome. One of the immediate consequences of the war was the flocking of millions of young people, many of them veterans taking advantage of the GI Bill of Rights, to our universities, in numbers for which those settings were hardly prepared. A large number entered the natural sciences as well as the social sciences, which, in keeping with the zeitgeist, were embarked on the "scientification" of their fields. Science was not only in the air but in the warp and woof of institutional programs and public policy. Financial support seemed no problem. If America was to capitalize on the past achievements and future potential of science, it was in its self-interest to insure a steady flow of people into scientific fields. It was not long before some scientists began to be concerned with two related questions, based on acute observation of the public school. One was less a question than a conclusion: the science curriculum in our schools was scandalously outmoded and inadequate. The term "scientific illiteracy" began to gain currency. The other question was: how do we reform that curriculum so that from the beginning of schooling, and in ways appropriate to their developmental levels, children are "taught" what science is about and how to think in logical-scientific ways?[2]

That question, of course, had unusual salience for psychology, especially child psychology, which was a fast-growing field. This is not to say that psychologists were interested in the teaching of science in the classroom, because for the most part they were not. What they were interested in is how the child cognitively grasps and transacts with its surround, how it forms concepts and relationships, how thinking develops, how objectivity is attained. These and similar questions were central to Piaget's work. Whereas before the war Piaget had received little attention—he "only" talked to children, asked questions, offered no quantified data, speculated much—after the war he came into his own, so that by the early 1950s he began to become the dominant, indeed the

2. I put quotes around "taught" because the critics made the same mistake that characterizes art education: starting with and requiring the child to conform to predetermined content and goals. Between the children and the teacher is a curriculum, and the task of the teacher is "to put that curriculum into the students." In some magical way, the teachers, whom the critics said were part of the problem and not the solution, would make the curriculum interesting to and productive for students. It has been a near total disaster. The reasons are many, but one has to do with the question-asking phenomenon in the classroom I discussed earlier. The classroom is no place where children can ask their questions about the natural and social worlds. The interested reader may wish to consult my *Schooling in America* (1983).

towering, figure in child development. As Dr. Aaron Hershkowitz said to me decades ago: "Piaget is tailor-made for a society that puts the highest value on logical thinking and the scientific endeavor. If you want a society of scientists, then Piaget is obviously relevant. If you want a society of artists, it is quite another story." And that is the point: ours is not a society that highly values or rewards artistic activity and development. It is not only that artistic activity takes a poor second place to scientific activity. It is that artistic activity is so frequently seen as the antithesis of scientific activity: a mystical, intuitive, less socially worthy activity before which we must "throw up our hands." It is to Piaget's credit—as the quote cited earlier in this chapter attests—that he recognized that artistic activity and its development were important but devalued issues in psychology.

That recognition by Piaget is not surprising because central to his life task was how we come to *know* our world, and knowing involved far more than what we colloquially mean by knowledge. The process of knowing, at every stage in development, is one in which a curious organism internally represents and explains something in the "out there." It is not, as Dewey pointed out almost a century ago, a process explainable by *an* external stimulus evoking *a* response. It is, in Piaget's terms, a process of assimilation and accommodation: the "out there" is and becomes a feature of an internal "schema" that then impacts upon the "out there." And, crucially, the "in there" and the "out there" have form and structure. That is seen most clearly in Piaget's studies of how children conceive of and represent space and spatial relationships, how those conceptions and representations change with experience over time. But Piaget was not primarily interested in these conceptions and representations for what they suggest about creativity and artistic activity. His real interest was the origins and development of logical-scientific schemes for understanding and coping with one's world. How the human organism becomes able to take distance from concrete perceptions and the qualities of palpable objects, to refrain from being taken in, so to speak, by what hits one's eye, to learn to use abstract principles for the purpose of understanding and coping with the implicit (not explicit) nature of one's world—these were the questions Piaget addressed and which he so brilliantly illuminated. As someone once said to me: "If I had to say in a nutshell what Piaget was about, it would be to explain how we come in our society to deal not with the world of appearances but with its underlying realities, the underlying principles." Artistic activity starts and ends with the world of appearances, and in between those points is a process no less cognitively complex and developmental in nature than the cognitive schemes Piaget described. But in a world that places such great store in acquiring the capacity to think logically, abstractly, scientifically, artistic activity is a second-class activity.

The challenge of art to psychology is really twofold. Art challenges the ways in which psychology conceives of human potential. No psychologist—indeed, no reasonable person—would defend a psychology that did not distinguish between what people are and what people can be, what people do and what they can be helped to do. In brief, as a scientific enterprise, psychology cannot accept the world of appearances, and in many respects it does not. This is why, for example, no issue has aroused and continues to arouse as much controversy as that centering on the role of nature and nurture, heredity and environment, potential and performance. And the passion that issue engenders should occasion no surprise because where one stands in regard to it has enormous consequences for social and educational policy and practice. No one is in doubt that there is a lot at stake!

An obvious feature of the controversy is how suffused psychological theory is with the culture in which it is embedded. Freud, Piaget, Watson, Skinner: the substance and impact of their theories are not "culture-free." If they sought "laws" that were universal in scope, the conceptual web in which they were embedded bore the stamps of era, place, and culture. And therein lies the second aspect of the challenge of art to psychology. To what extent and in what ways is psychology's relative disinterest in artistic activity (and creativity generally) symptomatic of an unreflective acceptance of a worldview in which the developmental significances of that activity either are hardly recognized or are seen as the opposite of universal? Was psychology's enthusiastic embracing of Piaget's seminal contributions in the post–World War II era not only a reflection of the times but, at the same time, an unfortunate reinforcement of a very narrow view of human potential, a view I believe Piaget did not share?

The nature and implications of these questions contain a mammoth obstacle to their recognition and serious discussion, let alone their acceptance. Today, we can read Freud and see much of ourselves in much that he describes. And the same is true when we read Piaget. To use an overused term, we can identify with what they have written. But that is not the case when we read about artistic activity and artists because most of us see ourselves as ciphers in regard to artistic activity.

We have been schooled to regard artistic activity as foreign to our abilities, and we content ourselves with trying to fathom and appreciate what our world has told us is "really" art. That artistic activity is a normal human attribute (the stifling of which robs people of modes of creative expression and impoverishes their sense of agency in and on their worlds) strikes most people as, at best, wish-fulfillment or utopianism run riot—or, at worst, a denial of what is obvious in our quotidian and personal worlds. Artistic activity is something special and few people have that something. It is a something with which we cannot identify. As I said earlier, one of the many ways in which we can characterize human history is as a saga of the underestimation of human potential, for good and bad.

Only one psychologist saw and addressed the challenge. Unfortunately, Dewey's *Art as Experience* is a nonbook in American psychology. I have yet to meet a psychologist (or any other social scientist) who has read it, and most have never even heard of it. Dewey is very far from the mainstream of American psychology. Like William James, he has been categorized as a philosopher and, therefore, not relevant to psychology as science. Worse yet, he is thought of as an educator, lowering his status further. What has gone unrecognized is that Dewey, far more than James, was an experimentalist and developmentalist who sought to understand how the capacities of people are affected by social context, societal values, and social institutions. Dewey did not create the lab school at the University of Chicago in 1896 because of a narrow interest in education but as a way of testing his conceptions of what children were and could be in his society. *Art as Experience* contains little or nothing about education in general and schools in particular. But like so much in his earlier writings, the book goes straight to the core question: how do we, and how should we, conceive of the capacities of the human organism?

In the next chapter I shall summarize Dewey's analysis in relation to the questions: what is and what is not art, and who is and who is not an artist? As we shall see, Dewey was a destroyer of traditional dichotomies.

5 ◆ DEWEY'S ART
AS EXPERIENCE

On the first page of the first chapter Dewey states: "When artistic objects are separated from both conditions of origin and operation in experience, a wall is built around them that renders almost opaque their general significance, with which aesthetic experience deals. Art is remitted to a separate realm, where it is cut off from association with the materials and aims of every other form of human effort, undergoing, and achievement." The task, Dewey goes on to say, is

> to restore continuity between the refined and intensified forms of experience that are works of art and the everyday events, doings, and sufferings that are universally recognized to constitute experience. Mountain peaks do not float unsupported; they do not even just rest upon the earth. They are the earth in one of its manifest operations. It is the business of those who are concerned with the theory of the earth, geographers and geologists, to make this fact evident in its various implications. The theorist who would deal philosophically with fine art has a like task to accomplish.
>
> If one is willing to grant this position, even if only by way of temporary experiment, he will see that there follows a conclusion at first sight surprising. In order to understand the meaning of artistic products, we have to forget them for a time, to turn aside from them and have recourse to the ordinary forces and conditions of experience that we do not usually regard as esthetic. We must arrive at the theory of art by means of a detour. For theory is concerned with understanding, insight, not without exclamations of admiration, and stimulation of that emotional outburst often called admiration. It is quite possible to enjoy flowers in their colored form and delicate fragrance without knowing anything about plants theoretically. But if one sets out to understand the flowering of plants, he is committed to finding out something about the interactions of soil, air, water and sunlight that condition the growth of plants. (P. 3)

Dewey does not leave the reader in doubt about his seriousness in claiming that what we ordinarily mean by artistic activity (its products or appreciation of them) contains features characteristic of everyday experience:

> In order to understand the esthetic in its ultimate and approved forms, one must begin with it in the raw; in the events and scenes that hold the attentive eye and ear of man, arousing his interest and affording him enjoyment as he looks and listens: the sights that hold the crowd—the fire-engine rushing by; the machines excavating enormous holes in the earth; the human-fly climbing the steeple-side; the men perched high in air on girders, throwing and catching red-hot bolts. The sources of art in human experience will be learned by him who sees how the tense grace of the ball-player infects the onlooking crowd; who notes the delight of the housewife in tending her plants, and the intent interest of her goodman in tending the patch of green in front of the house; the zest of the spectator in poking the wood burning on the hearth and in watching the darting flames and crumbling coals. These people, if questioned as to the reason for their actions, would doubtless return reasonable answers. The man who poked the sticks of burning wood would say he did it to make the fire burn better; but he is none the less fascinated by the colorful drama of change enacted before his eyes and imaginatively partakes of it. He does not remain a cold spectator. What Coleridge said of the reader of poetry is true in its way of all who are happily absorbed in their activities of mind and body: "The reader should be carried forward, not merely or chiefly by the mechanical impulse of curiosity, not by a restless desire to arrive at the final solution, but by the pleasurable activity of the journey itself."
>
> The intelligent mechanic engaged in his job, interested in doing well and finding satisfaction in his handiwork, caring for his materials and tools with genuine affection, is artistically engaged. The difference between such a worker and the inept and careless bungler is as great in the shop as it is in the studio. Oftentimes the product may not appeal to the esthetic sense of those who use the product. The fault, however, is oftentimes not so much with the worker as with the conditions of the market for which his product is designed. Were conditions and opportunities different, things as significant to the eye as those produced by earlier craftsmen would be made. (P. 4)

Dewey had an amazing knowledge and grasp of human history and its diverse cultures. So it is not surprising when he says:

> Bodily scarification, waving feathers, gaudy robes, shining ornaments of gold and silver, of emerald and jade, formed the contents of esthetic arts, and, presumably, without the vulgarity of class exhibitionism that attends their analogues today. Domestic utensils, furnishings of tend and house, rugs, mats, jars, pots, bows, spears, were wrought with such delighted care that today we hunt them out and give them places of honor in our art museums. Yet in their own time and place, such things were enhancements of the

processes of everyday life. Instead of being elevated to a niche apart, they belonged to display of prowess, the manifestation of group and clan membership, worship of gods, feasting and fasting, fighting, hunting, and all the rhythmic crises that punctuate the stream of living.

Dancing and pantomime, the sources of the art of the theater, flourished as part of religious rites and celebrations. Musical art abounded in the fingering of the stretched string, the beating of the taut skin, the blowing with reeds. Even in the caves, human habitations were adorned with colored pictures that kept alive to the senses experiences with the animals that were so closely bound with the lives of humans. Structures that housed their gods and the instrumentalities that facilitated commerce with the higher powers were wrought with especial fineness. But the arts of the drama, music, painting, and architecture thus exemplified had no peculiar connection with theaters, galleries, museums. They were part of the significant life of an organized community. (P. 6)

The first of the several themes Dewey discusses is that what we have been taught to regard as artistic activity, far from being unique or special, arises from and builds on "ordinary" experience. And by experience Dewey means that which intensifies the sense of immediate living, that which has a starting and end point linked by a transaction between "inside and outside," allowing us to say that we have had *an* experience. "It is mere ignorance that leads to the supposition that connection of art and esthetic perception with experience signifies a lowering of their significance and dignity. Experience in the degree in which it *is* experience is heightened vitality. Instead of signifying being shut up within one's own private feelings and sensations, it signifies active and alert commerce with the world; at its height it signifies complete interpenetration of self and the world of objects and events. Instead of signifying surrender to caprice and disorder, it affords our sole demonstration of a stability that is not stagnation but is rhythmic and developing. Because experience is the fulfillment of an organism in its struggles and achievements in a world of things, it is art in germ. Even in its rudimentary forms, it contains the promise of that delightful perception which is esthetic experience" (p. 19).

Why, Dewey asks, is there hostile reaction to a conception of art that connects it with the activities of an ordinary creature in its environment? That hostility, Dewey asserts, is a "pathetic, even a tragic commentary on life as it is ordinarily lived. Only because life is usually so stunted, aborted, slack, or heavy-laden is the idea entertained that there is some inherent antagonism between the process of normal living and the creation and enjoyment of works of esthetic art." Put in another way, the fact that so many ordinary people so infrequently have *an* experience, leading lives seemingly devoid of pleasure consequent to perceptual and motoric commerce with their world, lacking active purpose and the sense of productive personal agency, gives us no warrant to conclude that these people always lacked the spark of artistic activity.

For Dewey, an experience is far more than "doing and undergoing in alternation but consists of them in relationship. To put one's hand in the fire that consumes it is not necessarily to have an experience. *The action and its consequence must be joined in perception. The relationship is what gives meaning; to grasp it is the objective of all intelligence*" (p. 44, italics mine). The perception of a relationship between what is done and what is undergone constitutes the work of intelligence. "The artist is controlled in the process of working by his grasp of the connection between what he has already done and what he is to do next." At every step in the process the painter, Dewey notes, "must consciously undergo the effect of his every brushstroke or he will not be aware of what he is doing and where his work is going. Moreover, he has to see each particular connection of doing and undergoing in relation to the whole he seeks to produce. To apprehend such relations is to think, and is one of the most exacting modes of thought" (p. 45). Dewey views as obviously "absurd" the idea that the artist does not think as intently and penetratingly as the scientist.

Dewey uses the term *impulsion* to designate a movement of the whole organism outward and forward. Impulsions, especially in young children, are starting points for an experience but do not necessarily result in a complete experience unless they are woven as strands into an activity that calls the whole self into play. Giving unbridled vent to impulsions as often as not short-circuits having an experience:

There are storms of passion that break through barriers and that sweep away whatever intervenes between a person and something he would destroy. There is activity, but not, from the standpoint of the one acting, expression. An onlooker may say, "What a magnificent expression of rage!" But the enraged being is only raging, quite a different matter from expressing anger. Or, again, some spectator may say "How that man is expressing his own dominant character in what he is doing or saying." But the last thing the man in question is thinking of is to express his character; he is only giving way to a fit of passion. Again the cry or smile of an infant may be expressive to mother or nurse and yet not be an act of expression of the baby. To the onlooker it is an expression because it tells something about the state of the child. But the child is only engaged in doing something directly, no more expressive from his standpoint than is breathing or sneezing—activities that are also expressive to the observer of the infant's condition. (P. 61)

Dewey's concept of experience refers to a process that is developmental in nature and has the effect of in some way transforming the perception of the relations between the "in there" and the "out there." It has a starting point that builds on prior experience and has a direction or a controlling quality that determines when and what the culminating point will be. But it is developmental in a larger sense in that the process is central to understanding how a neonate becomes a thinking person. And the concept exposes how obfuscating, distracting, and misleading it is to view artistic activity as something special, a mode of doing, undergoing, and appreciating that requires its own psychology. Just as we do not need one theory to explain the workings of the oxygen atom and another to explain the helium atom, we do not need a special theory to explain artistic activity. Of course, there are differences between artistic and scientific doing and thinking, just as there are differences between the oxygen and helium atoms, but to a psychologist like Dewey it is their commonalities and points of identity that illuminate the workings of the human mind. And those commonalities inhere in the nature and structure of *an* experience. What is art? Dewey answers the question in two ways. The negative way is that what one sees in museums and galleries is a select, distorted, culturally prejudiced sample of the products of artistic activity. The positive way is that artistic activity, as doing or appreciating, is a universal feature of human experience reflecting a need for, indeed a hunger for, experience pleasing to the senses. It is not an activity foreign to the biologically intact organism. And because of those answers, Dewey does not have to raise and discuss the question: who is an artist?

There is a second theme in *Art as Experience* that Dewey discusses, albeit briefly, in the first and last chapters. To anyone familiar with the corpus of Dewey's writings it would be surprising if this theme had been absent. It is a theme alluded to earlier in this chapter in connection with Dewey's discussion of why there is such resistance to connecting artistic activity to daily experience. That hostility is a *"pathetic, even a tragic commentary on life as it is ordinarily lived. Only because life is usually so stunted, aborted, slack, or heavy-laden is the idea entertained that there is some inherent antagonism between the process of normal living and the creation and enjoyment of works of esthetic art"* (italics mine). Those words are as succinct an expression of Dewey the social historian, analyst, and critic as one will find. Their meaning and force derive from Dewey's analysis of how the rise of capitalism and its market economies changed worldviews, the basis of social relationships, and people's relationship to work. His position on these matters in regard to art and artistic activity can be summarized briefly. The rise of the impersonal market economy resulted in an individualism that weakened, and frequently destroyed, the fabric of communal living. Whereas previously the meaning of art derived solely from its communal functions (such as religion) and could have no significances beyond its shared communal ones, the rise of the impersonal market weakened that intimate social connection. The separation of art and the artist from their communal moorings was but a reflection of how people were being separated psychologically and socially from each other. Whereas works of art had had indigenous, communal meanings and functions, they now acquired a new status: "that of being specimens of fine art and nothing else":

> The growth of capitalism has been a powerful influence in the development of the museum as the proper home for works of art, and in the promotion of the idea that they are apart from the common life. The nouveaux riches, who are an important by-product of the capitalist system, have felt especially bound to surround themselves with works of fine art which, being rare, are also costly. Generally speaking, the typical collector is the typical capitalist. For evidence of good standing in the realm of higher culture, he amasses paintings, statuary, and artistic bijoux, as his stocks and bonds certify to his standing in the economic world.
>
> Not merely individuals, but communities and nations put their cultural good taste in evidence by building opera houses, galleries and museums. These show that a community is not wholly absorbed in material wealth, because it is willing to spend its gains in patronage of art. It erects these buildings and collects their contents as it now builds a cathedral. These things reflect and establish superior cultural status, while their segregation from the common life reflects the fact that they are not part of a native and spontaneous culture. They are a kind of counterpart of a holier-than-thou attitude, exhibited not toward persons as such but toward the interests and occupations that absorb most of the community's time and energy. (P. 8)

The transformations that created a gulf between producer and consumer had the consequence of creating a chasm "between ordinary and esthetic experience." If Dewey's *Art as Experience* does not dwell long on some of the consequences of the rise of capitalism, it is because his main objective is to expose how theories of art and artistic activity became captive of that rise:

> My purpose, however, is not to engage in an economic interpretation of the history of the arts, much less to argue that economic conditions are either invariably or directly relevant to perception and enjoyment, or even to interpretation of individual works of art. It is to indicate that theories which isolate art and its appreciation by placing them in a realm of their own, disconnected from other modes of experiencing, are not inherent in the subject-matter but arise because of specifiable extraneous conditions. Embedded as they are in institutions and in habits of life, these conditions operate effectively because they work so unconsciously. Then the theorist assumes they are embedded in the nature of things. Nevertheless, the influence of these conditions is not confined to theory. As I have already indicated, it deeply affects the practice of living, driving away esthetic perceptions that are necessary ingredients of happiness, or reducing them to the level of compensating transient pleasurable excitations. (P. 10)

The theories are *"not inherent in the subject matter but arise because of specifiable extraneous conditions."* The ahistorical, culturally socialized theorist, no less than almost everyone else, is unaware that putting art in a realm of its own has been conditioned by a particular social-economic-intellectual history. And that unawareness permits the theorist to assume that he or she is dealing with "the nature of things," insensitive to how "the nature of things" has undergone transformations.

Why was it so important to Dewey to write a book establishing a connection between a conception of fine art and ordinary experience? His answer is that it will help us better to understand the factors and forces "that favor the normal development of common human activities into matters of artistic value. It will also be able to point out those conditions that arrest its normal growth. . . . It is safe to say that a philosophy of art is sterilized unless it makes us aware of the function of art in relation to other modes of experience, and unless it indicates why this function is so inadequately realized, and unless it suggests the conditions under which the office would be successfully performed" (p. 12).

Although it is a nonbook in American psychology, *Art as Experience* is one of the most direct challenges to that field. It is challenging in the same way that his 1899 presidential address to the American Psychological Association was challenging. In that address he discussed and vehemently criticized a conception of education that separated the child in school from his or her nonschool world, the school world from the "ordinary" world, abstractions from their origins in concrete experience, individual from social group experience; a conception that in practice ignores and stifles the child's curiosity, interests, and capacities. As I said earlier, Dewey did not start the lab school at the University of Chicago because of any narrow interest in pedagogy. What he sought to explore and demonstrate was how what passed for "the nature of things" in our schools was a product of social history and not inherent in the subject matter of education. The way things are is not the way things can and should be. *Art as Experience* presents a similar challenge. In destroying the dichotomy between what is art and what is non-art, and exposing it as a social-historical construction, in emphasizing the commonalities between "fine art" and ordinary experience, and in giving us a vision of what the human organism is normally capable of, Dewey is criticizing a psychology that underestimates the organism's capacities and the extent to which theorists and their theories always run the risk of being unwitting products of time, place, and era.

A third theme in Dewey's book is the "restorative" function of artistic activity: the satisfaction that comes from transforming one's self and something in the "out there" into an organized form that has individuality, a personal stamp. That transformation, which may occur in the process of making or appreciating, involves, as do many other true experiences, struggle and even suffering, but at the conclusion of the process there is satisfaction from the feeling of crafted individuality, that one has organized and been organized creatively. Only those who have never read Dewey on education can hold the view that Dewey started the cult of mindless expressiveness. Dewey distinguished clearly between expression that was unformed and unforming, and expression involving a unity among all cognitive capacities. And nowhere does Dewey make that distinction clearer than in *Art and Experience*. The absence, total or relative, of that restorative function in the lives of most people says far less to Dewey about human capacity than it does about social-historical changes whose effect has been to consign most people to an impoverished psychological existence. Dewey never denies that there are or may be constitutional differences or predispositions in regard to the diverse forms of artistic expression. He does deny the belief that such expression is inherently special, that some people are capable of it and others (*most* others) are not. The capacity for artistic activity, like the capacity to have *an* experience, is a normal attribute or capacity that, first and last, requires opportunity, support, and understanding.

It should now be obvious why toward the end of his life Dewey so willingly agreed to write a foreword for Schaefer-Simmern's *Unfolding of Artistic Activity.* For one thing, Dewey praises Schaefer-Simmern for going beyond a theory "to testing and confirmation in work carried out over many years and with a variety of groups." Like Schaefer-Simmern, Dewey started his lab school to wed theory and practice. For Dewey, theory emerges from practice and in turn returns to practice. Dewey goes on in his foreword to call attention to Schaefer-Simmern's emphasis on "individuality as the creative factor in life's experiences":

> An immense amount has been said and written about the individual and about individuality. Too much of it, however, is vitiated by setting up what these words stand for as if it were something complete in itself in isolation. Here it is seen and consistently treated as the life factor that varies from the previously given order, and that in varying transforms in some measure that from which it departs, even in the very act of receiving and using it. This creativity is the meaning of artistic activity—which is manifested not just in what are regarded as the fine arts, but in all forms of life that are not tied down to what is established by custom and convention. In re-creating them in its own way, it brings refreshment, growth, and satisfying joy to one who participates. (P. ix)

Dewey's words are as succinct a summary of *Art as Experience* as one can make. In other contexts and by other writers, the phrase "the life factor" may strike one as vague, mushy, and up-in-the-clouds. But Dewey is extraordinarily clear that the life factor is the normal human attribute that allows us to depart from a previous given order and to forge a new one. It is the attribute that, despite the process of socialization and its goal to maximize continuity of and conformity to the established order, ensures individuality.

Dewey was a gestaltist long before the German gestaltists formulated their position and had an impact on American psychology. That is why he stresses in his foreword the significance of Schaefer-Simmern's evidence:

> Accompanying this principle, or rather inseparable from it, is the evidence that artistic activity is an undivided union of factors which, when separated, are called physical, emotional, intellectual, and practical—these last in the sense of doing and making. These last, however, are no more routine and dull than the emotional stir is raw excitation. Intelligence is the informing and formative factor throughout. It is manifested in that keen and lively participation of the sense organs in which they are truly organs of constructive imagination. Intelligence is also manifested in the organizing activity of which aesthetic form is the result. But nothing could be further away from

that conformity to fixed rules, disguised as principles and standards, which is too often taken to be the function of "rationality." Escape from the one-sidedness which attends many philosophies of sense, of reason, of bodily or physical action, of emotion, and of doing and making—distinguishes the work reported upon in the following pages. In their place there is constant observation of the wholeness of life and personality in which activity becomes artistic.

Because of this wholeness of artistic activity, because the entire personality comes into play, artistic activity which is art itself is not an indulgence but is refreshing and restorative, as is always the wholeness that is health. There is no inherent difference between fullness of activity and artistic activity; the latter is one with being fully alive. Hence, it is not something possessed by a few persons and setting them apart from the rest of mankind, but is the normal or natural human heritage. Its spontaneity is not a gush, but is the naturalness proper to all organized energies of the live creature. Persons differ greatly in their respective measures. *But there is something the matter, something abnormal, when a human being is forbidden by external conditions from engaging in that fullness according to his own measure, and when he finds it diverted by these conditions into unhealthy physical excitement and appetitive indulgence.*

Normally and naturally, artistic activity is the way in which one may "gain in the strength and stature, the belief in his own powers, and the self-respect, which makes artistic activity constructive in the growth of personality." It is this fact that distinguishes the demonstrations conducted by Professor Schaefer-Simmern. They take place in a particular field of activity as every form of experimental demonstration must do. But through that field, as well as in it, there is convincing thoroughgoing demonstration that activity which is artistic extends beyond all subjects conventionally named "The Fine Arts." For it provides the pattern and model of the full and free growth of personality and of full life activity, wherever it occurs, bringing refreshment and, when needed, restoration. (Pp. ix–x)

The sentences I italicized are as clear an example as one will find of Dewey's emphasis on external conditions (social, economic, political, and intellectual) that obscure or inhibit or bury what is distinctively a human potential.

I regard what Dewey does *not* discuss in his foreword as not less significant, perhaps more significant, than what he does say. I refer specifically to the fact that two of Schaefer's chapters, constituting one-third of his book, demonstrate and discuss the artistic productions of people who either are mentally retarded or have a low IQ. That they were by cultural and professional standards *sub*ordinary people was of no special importance to Dewey. For him, intelligence was a far more encompassing concept than what we have been schooled to regard as intelligence or intelligent behavior. Intelligence tests do not sample the "life factor." What people are and do, as we conventionally explain *and* judge them, should never be confused with what people can be and do. In this respect, ironically, Dewey's position differs in no wise from Skinner's in *Walden Two*. And is it not ironic that Skinner, the most influential behaviorist of the contemporary era, proclaims, like Dewey, that artistic activity is a uniquely human attribute unfulfilled in most because of "external conditions"? It is also ironic that it was Dewey—who "once" was a psychologist and then "became" a philosopher and educator—and not Skinner who has given us the most comprehensive and penetrating psychological analysis of artistic activity as attribute and process.

One more irony. Skinner (for whom I have great respect) was and is the William James Professor of Psychology (emeritus) at Harvard. Dewey's *Art as Experience* was based on his William James lectures at Harvard. But, in my opinion, it was Dewey more than Skinner who carried on the Jamesian tradition. Dewey did for artistic activity what James did for religious experience. *Art as Experience* is more of a non-book in American psychology than James's *Varieties of Religious Experience*, a matter of degree. It is not happenstance that the word *experience* is common to both titles. Both men sought to describe and explain certain forms of experience: their origins, forms, and functions. And in the seeking, neither of these men made the mistake of regarding these experiences as "special," as having no kinship to ordinary experience. Quite the contrary, they illuminated the obvious: their kinship.

In the previous chapter, I noted the observation, made by many, that the creativity of preschoolers seems to languish or evaporate during the school years, reappearing in some (a few, relatively speaking) during adolescence. That would hardly have surprised Dewey. Indeed, that observation is both implicit and explicit in his writings on education. But what would be the status of that observation if, as Schaefer-Simmern demonstrated, people had the opportunity to engage in some form of artistic activity—ordinary people, children and adults? Let us assume for the moment (I shall treat this at length in a later chapter) that the opportunity will be in conformity with the individual's interest, experience, and artistic level—that is, it will not be a "memory game," or a copy of external reality, or expression as catharsis, or technique as sheer skill. What if, in Dewey's words, people were "not forbidden by external conditions from engaging in that fullness according to [their] own measure"?

These are not questions that have easy answers. It would be more accurate to say that we are in no position even to imagine answers because intuitively we know that the implications of these questions are both strange and vast, challenging as they do our worldview not only of what people use and can be but also of what society is and should be.

It is fitting to close this chapter with the observations of an art teacher in Westport, Connecticut. His account was stimulated by a presentation I had made about, among other things, the question-asking behavior of schoolchildren. "May I tell you about something I have done a number of times with kindergarteners and high school seniors? I ask the kindergarteners to raise their hands if they can read. I then ask if they can work with numbers. Then I ask if they can write. At best one or two of them will raise their hands; usually none does. When I then ask them if they can draw or make pictures, everyone raises their hand. Now, when I have done that same thing with high school seniors, each of them raises his hand in regard to reading, writing, and numbers. In regard to drawing and making pictures, it has been rare that anyone raises his or her hand."

6 ◆ ARTISTIC ACTIVITY,

GHETTO CHILDREN, AND

NURSING HOME RESIDENTS

The first question a scientific researcher should ask is, what evidence exists—evidence that would stand up in the court of science—that all people are capable of artistic activity *and* development according to their own measure? This hypothesis demands serious study. After all, what is at stake is no more and no less than our understanding of the human mind and our society. The hypothesis suggests that the conventional wisdom is no more than that: conventional.

The evidence is scanty but compelling. That it is scanty is not surprising, given the fact that artistic activity is so far from the mainstream of American psychology. I shall not attempt anything like a comprehensive review of the evidence. Rather, I will briefly discuss a few efforts that I have found most interesting. One such effort I have discussed in detail in chapter 3, on Schaefer-Simmern's *Unfolding of Artistic Activity*. A related effort was by Kerwin Whitnah, an artist and teacher who studied with Schaefer-Simmern. Several years after Schaefer-Simmern's death, Mr. Whitnah visited me in order to show me what his students (mostly school-aged children) had done. He came with a projector and several hundred slides. Over a period of several hours he must have shown me the step-by-step artistic development of at least a dozen children. They were "ordinary" children, not screened by any test of artistic talent. His presentation reminded me of slides of histological sections of the brain, allowing one to see small changes culminating in big ones. Like Schaefer-Simmern (and like any good histologist), he noted small changes in the organization of form where most of us see nothing, changes signifying an ongoing transformation.

In regard to Schaefer-Simmern's work I had one gnawing question:

was it replicable? Could somebody else apply his ideas with similarly impressive results? Mr. Whitnah's presentation was reassuring. But Mr. Whitnah is a teacher, not an investigator obliged to publish his findings. Undoubtedly, others who studied with Schaefer-Simmern could show comparable achievements. And I have no doubt that many other teachers, not even acquainted with Schaefer-Simmern's work, possess evidence confirming the hypothesis that artistic activity and development are human attributes that, when given the appropriate contextual opportunity, not only are realized but also transform the individual's sense of self and his or her world. The psychological consequences of such realization can be enormous. For those who have heretofore seen themselves as uncreative, the consequences can be "restorative." For children of any age the consequences can be no less than an experience of unfolding and growth, an experience of discovery. I shall return to these points in a while.

Let us for the moment leave the arena of visual art for that of poetry. As in the case of visual art, poetic artistry is conventionally viewed as something special. And if my extensive experience in schools is typical, one must conclude that the idea that children are poets is far more alien to the culture of schools than the idea that they are visual artists. Some schools make provision for teachers of visual art to visit so that students may spend an hour or so a week in such activity, although in an economic crunch, the teacher of art is among the first to go. I have been in hundreds of schools—urban, suburban, rural, rich, poor, white, black, Hispanic, Oriental, and mixed in composition—and I cannot recall one that budgeted for the teaching of poetry. That may be a blessing in disguise, because unless such teaching starts with the Schaefer-Simmern conception of "unfolding" of artistic activity, it obscures what it allegedly seeks to illuminate.

So I turn now to a book: *Wishes, Lies, and Dreams* (1970) by Kenneth Koch, a poet of international stature and a professor of creative writing at Columbia. Koch decided to teach poetry at an elementary school (P.S. 61) in New York City made up largely of black and Hispanic children. "I was curious to see what could be done for children's poetry," he writes. "I knew some things about teaching adults to write. . . . But I didn't know about children. Adult writers had read a lot, wanted to be writers, and were driven by all the usual forces writers are driven by. I knew how to talk to them, how to inspire them, how to criticize their work. What to say to an eight-year-old with no commitment to literature?" (p. 2). Not only what to say but what to do to gain that *willing* commitment without which having an artistic experience is nearly impossible. Koch's book contains more than three hundred pages, most of which are devoted to the works of these children, from their earliest to their latest efforts. I must leave it to the interested reader to examine and judge what Koch and these children accomplished over a period of several months. "I usually went to the school two or three afternoons a week and taught three forty-minute classes. Toward the end I taught more often, because I had become so interested and because I knew I was going to write about it and wanted as much experience as possible." (p. 2). Let me summarize the major points with which I think any reader of Koch's book would agree:

1. Koch came to his task already impressed with "how playful and inventive children's talk sometimes was. They said true things in fresh and surprising ways. . . . Some children's poetry was marvelous but most seemed uncomfortably imitative of adult poetry or else childishly cute. It seemed restricted somehow, and it obviously lacked the happy, creative energy of children's art. I wanted to find, if I could, a way for children to get as much from poetry as they did from painting" (pp. 2–3).

2. Two things needed to be avoided: (a) requiring the child to use forms of verbal relationships (like rhyming) that are difficult and confining, and (b) suggesting content of no personal significance to him or her. No less than Schaefer-Simmern, Koch understood the negative consequences of imitation.

3. One should not judge the poetry of children by its obvious differences from that of recognized adult poets. But Koch found early on that their poetry was similar in one crucial respect: both possessed form. The children's poems "were all innocence, elation, and intelligence. They were unified poems: it made sense where they started and where they stopped. And they had a lovely music" (p. 6). The children *were* poets. The seeds of artistry were there.

4. What occupied Koch in the earliest days, what required him to experiment, was not only how to interest children in constructing poems but how to help them overcome the mind-set that there were "right and wrong" ways of proceeding, a set that short-circuited imaginativeness. If anything is obvious in Koch's account, it is (again as in Schaefer-Simmern) the respect he had for what the children could do and his support and acceptance of what they did. He liberated their imaginativeness, not fearful that what they would write would be amorphous, verbal glob.

Some things about teaching children to write poetry I knew in advance, instinctively or from having taught adults, and others I found out in the classroom. Most important, I believe, is taking children seriously as poets. Children have a natural talent for writing poetry and anyone who teaches them should know that. Teaching really is not the right word for what takes place; it is more like permitting the children to discover something they already have. I helped them to do this by removing obstacles, such as the need to rhyme, and by encouraging them in various ways to get tuned in to their own strong feelings, to their spontaneity, their sensitivity, and their carefree inventiveness. At first I was amazed at how well the children wrote, because there was obviously not enough in what I had told them to begin to account for it. I remember that after I had seen the fourth-grade Wish Poems, I invited their teacher, Mrs. Wiener, to lunch in order to discover her "secret." I thought she must have told her students certain special things to make them write such good poems. But she had done no more than what I had suggested she do: tell the children to begin every line with "I wish," not to use rhyme, and to make the wishes real or crazy. There was one other thing: she had been happy and excited about their doing it, and she had expected them to enjoy it too.

I was, as I said, amazed, because I hadn't expected any grade-school children, much less fourth graders, to write so well so soon. I thought I might have some success with sixth graders, but even there I felt it would be best to begin with a small group who volunteered for a poetry workshop. After the fourth-grade Wish Poems, however, and after the Wish and Comparison Poems from the other grades, I realized my mistake. The children in all the grades, primary through sixth, wrote poems which they enjoyed and I enjoyed. Treating them like poets was not a case of humorous but effective diplomacy, as I had first thought; it was the right way to treat them because it corresponded to the truth. A little humor, of course, I left in. Poetry was serious, but we joked and laughed a good deal; it was serious because it was such a pleasure to write. Treating them as poets enabled me to encourage them and egg them on in a non-teacher-ish way—as an admirer and fellow worker rather than as a boss. It shouldn't be difficult for a teacher to share this attitude once it is plain how happily and naturally the students take to writing. (P. 24)

That young children happily and naturally take to writing will sound odd to those who have been frustrated in their attempts to improve educational outcomes and who end up blaming the victims—the students—for lack of interest and motivation.

5. The atmosphere in the classrooms during the few hours a week Koch was there contrasted dramatically with that in the modal class-

room with which we are all too familiar. The children were buoyant, eager, hard-working, *and* productive. Koch set the stage, he was the director, but he had no script. He knew what the ending of the drama should be, could be. The children were like actors seeking an author in a Pirandello play. They became the authors.

The force of Koch's book derives from the fact that the children were not "ordinary." They were black and Hispanic children in a ghetto school, not the usual setting for a project like his. The parallels with Schaefer-Simmern's work with mentally retarded individuals at the Southbury Training School are noteworthy.

Wishes, Lies, and Dreams was published in 1970. In 1977 Koch published *I Never Told Anybody*, more telling, poignant, and upsetting than the previous book. Chapter 1 begins with a poem by one of Koch's "students":

AUTUMN
Your leaves were yellow
And some of them were darker
And I picked them up
And carried them in the house
And put them in different vases

Your leaves sound different
I couldn't understand why
The leaves at that time of year
Had a rustle about them
And they would drop
At the least little thing
And I would listen
And pick up some of them.
                    Nadyl Catalfano

What Koch was about in this new experience is best put in his own words:

Last spring and summer I taught poetry writing at the American Nursing Home in New York City. The American Nursing Home is on the Lower East Side, at Avenue B and Fifth Street. I had about twenty-five students, and we met sixteen times, usually on Wednesday mornings for about an hour. The students were all incapacitated in some way, by illness or old age. Most were in their seventies, eighties, and nineties. Most were from the working class and had a limited education. They had worked as dry cleaners, messengers, short-order cooks, domestic servants. A few had worked in offices, and one had been an actress. The nursing home gave them safety and care and a few activities, and sometimes a trip to a show or a museum. They did little or no reading or writing. They didn't write poetry. . . .

The idea to teach old and ill people to write poetry had come to me as a result of an interesting hour I spent working with poetry at the Jewish Old Age Home in Providence, Rhode Island, and as a result of other hours, much less happy ones, I had spent as a visitor in nursing homes where nothing of that kind was going on. I wanted to see what could be done. I saw, even in their very difficult circumstances, possibilities for poetry—in the lives old people looked back on, in the time they had now to do that, and to think, and with a detachment hardly possible to them before. If, in the blankness and emptiness of a nursing home, they could write poetry, it would be a good thing—a serious thing for them to work at, something worth doing well and that engaged their abilities and their thoughts and feelings.

I sensed this possibility, but it was evident that the students I had at the American Nursing Home were removed from poetry and from the writing of poetry in many ways. None had written it before and none, I think, would have begun without the workshop. The workshop had to provide a bridge between what poetry was and what the people there were—old, ill, relatively uneducated, separated from their early lives, cautious about trying anything new, afraid people might think them "finished," worthless, unable to do things well. They also had a conception of poetry likely to make it impossible for them to write it well: the rhyming, metrical treatment of a certain "poetical" subject matter. Not only were they unfamiliar with poetry; they were quite out of the habit of learning, of sitting in a room and hearing something explained. These were problems aside from the physical ones. Some had recent memory loss, were forgetful, tended to ramble a little when they spoke. Everyone was ill, some people sometimes in pain. Depression was frequent. A few were blind, and some had serious problems in hearing. Several students had severe speech problems and were very difficult, at first, to understand. To be added to all this was their confinement within the walls and within the institutional regime of the nursing home; they had little chance to find, as poets usually do, fresh inspiration in new experiences, sights, and sounds. They lived without either the city or nature to inspire their feelings. Poetry, if they did write it, would have to come from memory and from what happened and from what we could help make happen right there in the nursing home. And almost none of our students were able to use their hands to write—either because of muscular difficulties or blindness.

Still, it is such a pleasure to say things, and such a special kind of pleasure to say them as poetry. I didn't, when I began, think much about the problems. I started, instead, with my feeling for the pleasure people could find in writing poetry, and assumed I could deal with any problems as they came up. My students, in fact, once given the chance to begin, were, in spite of all the difficulties, happy to be writing poems." (Pp. 3–6)

Most of this book, again not a small one, contains the poetry of these ill, old, dependent people. How Koch caught their interest, inspired, encouraged, and sustained them, is described briefly and clearly. His account of the nursing home and its patients is indubitably valid, unfortunately so. Some readers of Koch's first book may be hesitant to regard the children's poetry as "real." That hesitation will be minimal or absent in regard to the contents of the second book.

Koch, unlike Schaefer-Simmern, is no theorist. But the accomplishments of both are clear examples of the positive consequences of the self-fulfilling prophecy. Both start with the assumption that artistic activity is a normal human attribute and then proceed—first, by means of their manner, personal style, respect, patience, ingenuity, and bedrock belief in individuality of *ordered* expression, and, second, by avoiding pressures to conform to predetermined criteria of good and bad, right and wrong—to demonstrate the validity of the assumption. Or one can put it this way: both men asserted that we live in a world that does not believe—certainly does not take seriously—that artistic activity is a normal human attribute; that world demonstrates the negative consequences of the self-fulfilling dynamic. Schaefer-Simmern, far more explicitly than Koch, damns that world. Koch's criticisms are more implicit and muted.

Our society has scores of ways of keeping track of the nation's health and factors related to it: economic indices, educational test scores, demographic changes, evidence of disease, pollution, crime, pregnancies, abortions, and so forth. Unfortunately, but not surprisingly, we do not keep track of data that would throw light on—or call into question—the belief that artistic activity is a special activity of special people. In the absence of such data, I offer the observation that the post–World War II era has seen a significant increase across this country of programs and projects that offer people of all ages and backgrounds opportunities to engage in a wide variety of artistic activity. If I am right that the increase is startling, one cannot avoid asking: why has this happened in the post–World War II years? Obviously, no one proclaimed that we are all artists in some measure. But there have been some changes in worldview that I regard as part of the background behind that startling increase. I have discussed these changes in my book *Work, Aging, and Social Change* (1977). I should hasten to say that these changes do not represent a clean break with what came before, but rather a difference in emphasis.

The first such change, subtle but powerful, was that one can be many things in life and should expect to *be* and *do* many things in life. The decade of the depressive 1930s was followed by the turmoil of the war years, culminating in a victory promising a new world that seemed to demand a break with custom and tradition. All this changed people's expectations of themselves and of their society. That sequence of upheavals ushered in what I term the era of the redefinition of self. Everyone's life had been altered in some way to some degree. An old order had been found wanting, and a new one was fashioned. The new order was one of limitless opportunities for America and its people. If the substance and shape of that new order were by no means clear, if threatening clouds loomed on the national and international horizons, they seemed to reinforce rather than weaken the belief in the necessity for change.

It was not that people woke up one day and said: "I, we, must change." It was rather that they found themselves in a changed and changing world to which they could not be indifferent. Many people welcomed the change for what it meant for them, their individual futures, and their children. Their children would not be, must not be, constrained in their view of what they could be in life. Their children would fashion a new world and experience it in ways their parents had not. The goals of child rearing were mightily expanded. If it is hyperbole to say that many parents wanted their children to become Renaissance people, the hyperbole nevertheless contains a truth. It is, of course, not happenstance that terms like *self-realization, self-actualization, realizing one's potentials,* and *personal authenticity* gained popular currency. The concept of human potential underwent change, in terms of both substance and expectations. It is also not happenstance that traditional conceptions of human potential began to be militantly challenged by women, blacks, and other minorities. It was (and continues to be) an era of redefinition of self.

These changes were not, of course, taking place in a social vacuum. There was something akin to an explosion in the arts (the visual arts, music, dance, theater, literature, architecture, crafts) in terms of the number of groups, media attention, audiences, and financial support. Certainly in terms of size of audience (reached via television, for example) and financial support from foundations and governmental agencies, one can say that there has been an explosion. That is to say, the number of people actively participating in some form of artistic activity seems unexplainable by the increase in the population alone, which has doubled in the last four decades. And if one goes by the number of colleges and universities offering either courses or programs in the arts—or in the number that have established resident-artist positions—explosion is again not an inappropriate term. In regard to our public schools, however, the term explosion would be utterly inappropriate.

I came to New Haven shortly after the end of World War II. Until twenty years ago there were no more than three or four settings devoted to exhibiting the works of local artists. Today, there are at least twenty such places. The same rate of increase holds for other forms of artistic activity: theater, music, photography, film. I have not included Yale in this count, where one could spend a fair part of each week going to exhibits (formal and informal) and presentations of one or another kind of artistic activity. It was not that way when I came to Yale. If beginning in 1945 you were to plot the amount of newspaper space devoted to the "local" arts scene, there is no doubt that the shape of the curve would be upward. We now have two local weekly newspapers, at least one-third of whose pages are concerned with the arts. When in addition to its Sunday section on the arts, the *New York Times* added a bulky Friday supplement, it was testimony to the explosion. And, of course, when the federal government broke with tradition and created the National Endowment for the Arts, and a similar fund for the humanities, it testified further to the increase in the number of people engaging in artistic activity as well as taking the role of audience.

After serving for six years on the National Council on the Arts, the pianist Samuel Lipman wrote:

> By the early 1980s, the arts in America had reached a pinnacle of expansion and development unprecedented in our history. There is no need to cite statistics. It is enough to say that the operative word was *more*—more museums, more ballet companies, more modern-dance companies, more theater companies, more creative writing, more poetry, more symphony orchestras, more opera companies, more chamber music ensembles, more avant-garde groups, more exhibitions, more performances, more artists, more audiences, more patrons, more administrators, more press, more arts-conscious politicians. Everywhere—more, more, more.
>
> With more, of course, went bigger. Bigger groups, bigger companies, bigger institutions, bigger staffs, bigger earned income, bigger budgets, bigger subsidies, bigger commitments, and of course, bigger deficits. Perhaps the crowning confirmation of all this bigness was the happy news from the Census Bureau that in 1980 our artists, taken together as a class, amounted to at least one million souls, all struggling to create what at least some people some of the time might be open-minded enough to call art.[1]

1. *The New Criterion*, Sept. 1988: 6–7.

It is beyond my purposes to attempt a comprehensive explanation of the increase in the number of people engaged in some form of artistic activity, an activity through which they put their personal stamp on something in an ordered way. What I wish to emphasize is that the increase is both a direct and an indirect reflection of a change in world-view in the post–World War II era, not only about the nature of human potential but, no less significant, about the obligations of individuals to themselves: to experience and give expression to as many facets of their capacities as possible. That change in worldview has had repercussions far beyond the arena of art, of course. The United States Army has a television commercial that says: "Be all you can be, in the Army." In the post–World War II period as never before, people began to take that saying seriously.

One aspect of that change has yet to receive the attention it deserves. It is wrapped up in what I call the one-life, one-career imperative. What society has said, so to speak, to young people is: "Here is a smorgasbord of career opportunities, choose the one 'task' you will work at in your lifetime; you can be A or B, but you cannot be both." That is a message to which young people in the post–World War II era began to react negatively. The one-life, one-career imperative was on a collision course with "Be all that you can be." As our studies reported in *Work, Aging, and Social Change* suggest, young people resented and resisted the idea that they could be only one thing in life. There was more to them than that! They feared being "slotted," socialized into a narrow career path, unable seriously to exploit and test their diverse interests and capacities. They wanted to avoid what they perceived to be the straitjacket in which their parents found themselves.[2]

Although they did not verbalize it in this way, our interviewees feared being unable to give creative expression to what was in them—to put their unique mark in and on something. Career change has escalated markedly in the post–World War II era. The individual and social dynamics powering that escalation are very similar to those powering the increase in the number of people actively engaged in some form of artistic activity. When John Dewey spoke about the need for artistic activity, he was referring to the bedrock importance of ordered, creative expression in whatever one does, of being able to claim psychological

2. As I point out in that book, our society has made it easier (in the post–World War II era) to change marriage partners than to change careers, although their dynamics are identical, a fact of which our interviewees were aware.

ownership of an activity because it bears the unique stamp of the individual. No one who reads Dewey's *Art as Experience* will find it easy to regard artistic activity in the customary narrow, segregated, special way. Dewey wrote that book in the 1930s. If he did not predict the changes in worldview that would be wrought by World War II, his book contained a message that people born after the war began to take seriously, although many were completely unaware of what Dewey wrote.

But more than young people heard and responded to Dewey's message. Unless my observations are grossly atypical, there has been a startling increase in the number of older people who seek and decide to engage in some form of artistic activity, especially women. I have spoken to scores of such people, and one theme runs through their responses: "I have *always* wanted to do something creative, to *make* something that was *me, mine*. But I always saw myself as *uncreative*. Who was I to regard myself as an artist? As the years went by, as I began to ask what I wanted to do with my time and myself, I knew I had to do something about that empty feeling, that sense of unfulfillment." In most of these instances the decision to act was facilitated by a friend's action or by receiving a brochure of adult education courses offered in local schools or at a local "creative arts workshop." If their responses to my queries varied somewhat, there was no variation in the degree of satisfaction they voiced about engaging in artistic activity. In that respect they were no different from Koch's people, who had been languishing and slowly dying in a nursing home.

The title of Koch's book *I Never Told Anybody* in a way says it all: our need to express—literally, to press out of ourselves—in some ordered, configurated way our imagery, thoughts, feelings is early on inhibited and degraded. It is a need that then goes underground but is never completely extinguished, as Koch's book so poignantly demonstrates. It is inescapable that in children, that need hits us, so to speak, in the face. That after early childhood it begins to disappear, and to reappear in a few specially gifted adolescents says far less about artistic activity than it does about the force of culture and tradition and about a narrow, acultural psychology. A psychology that begins and ends with what people are, with what they appear to be, and only minimally and unimaginatively faces up to what people can be is at best an unproductive psychology and at worst an unwitting colluder with other forces in the underestimation of human potential. Artistic activity is special because of the challenge it represents to our conception of how human nature and nurture transact.

7 ◆ LEARNING TO BE A NON-ARTIST

When conversation lags on social occasions and you seek to enliven it, one ploy is to focus attention on defining certain words or concepts we use every day. Neurosis, schizophrenia, capitalism, intelligence, freedom, and culture are good words to choose, especially if representatives of the fields in which those concepts are crucial are present. It quickly becomes apparent that there is no relation between the clarity attained and the amount of adrenalin secreted.

No one is in doubt that these are important concepts in that they refer to phenomena, overt and covert, about which we make judgments that have very practical import for ourselves and others. Indeed, the conversation heats up because people come to see that these concepts determine individual and social action; that is, the facet of the concept that one person emphasizes ignores the consequences implied by another facet put forth by someone else. At the same time that each person seeks to articulate the essence of the concept, each becomes aware that one person's essence is another person's distraction or superficiality. The conversation usually terminates in agreement that the concept is horribly complex: important, fascinating, obviously divisive, and, perhaps, undefinable in comparison to such concepts as transportation, merchandising, or housing.

On one such occasion when I was present, the focus became: what is art? For the purpose of enlivening a conversation that question has few equals, especially if there is a significant range in age among the participants. In reality, the conversation was largely about what was good or bad art. For some the varieties of contemporary art were abominations, for others they were entrancing. For everyone art was important as aesthetic experience. These people spent a fair amount of their leisure time visiting galleries and museums, and within their means bought works of art. With one or two exceptions among the ten people, none regarded him or herself as having artistic talent or even inclination. In fact, at one time or another in the conversation, several people said, "I am not an artist but I know what I like." It was the hostess for the evening who quipped, "I cannot lay an egg but I surely know when I am eating a lousy one." Predictably, the evening ended with no one's opinion having been changed. At one point I tried to divert attention from aesthetic preference by asking if there were any commonalities in the artistic process regardless of the wildly different aesthetic reactions works of art engendered. But that attempt foundered on the belief that since none of us was an artist or had any artistic experience or talent, discussion of my question was impermissible.

This social occasion occurred around the time that this book began to germinate in my head, which accounts for the fact that on the way home I was struck first by the hostess's dogmatic assertion that she had no artistic talent, and second, by the way she had organized and furnished her home. I have no doubt that everyone at that gathering would have agreed that her home was a delight to the eye. It was not a big house, and no one feature stood out. The color scheme was muted and monochromatic, small sculptures and Indian baskets were arresting and yet unobtrusive, and the furniture was arranged so that one felt physically part of a group and not apart from it. You felt you were in a home and not a house. It was my wife who said shortly after we arrived: "This is a work of art." When we had entered, my reaction—a very fleeting one—was that this was a very "nice" house, and I let it go at that. On the way home I realized that my wife was absolutely correct. What to me was just "nice" was the end result of a very complicated process of thinking and experimentation, the goal of which was to give organized overt expression to an internal picture or imagery. In other words, it did not just happen, it did not spring full-blown like Athena from the head of Zeus, its parts were not just parts, the whole was indeed greater than the sum of its parts. It was a whole that expressed what its creator wanted to—and had to—*see*. She had to be satisfied that what she had done was *hers*. She possessed and was possessed by a visual conception she wanted to see "out there." At the urging of my wife I interviewed the hostess several days later. Could she describe to me the process by which she had accomplished her task? She looked at me rather blankly, not knowing where or how to start, puzzled by my interest.

The point of this anecdote is not that after a couple of hours I elicited from her introspections and retrospections that were in every respect similar to if not identical with what acclaimed artists, past and present, had said about their creative processes. The point is that it could never occur to her that what she had done was artistic, that *she* merited the label of artist. She was an "ordinary" person. As she vigorously said on that social occasion, she had no artistic inclinations, and who was she to talk about creativity? By the end of the interview she was still uncomfortable with the thought that she had been creative. At one point I asked her if she had ever thought of employing the services of an interior decorator. Yes, she said, she had brought in an interior decorator, but that had convinced her that she had to go her own way, that she had to live with *her* internal visual conception and not anyone else's. Imitation was not her cup of tea.

It is hard to exaggerate how imprisoned we are in a narrow conception of artistic activity. I said earlier that we are schooled to regard artistic activity as rare and special. I used the word *schooled* advisedly because in so many diverse ways we are told directly that artistic activity is a special gift, either inherited through genes or acquired through divine dispensation or unfathomable mystery. It could be argued that artistic activity, like most other human activities, is normally distributed in the population: a few engage in it to an extraordinary degree (the "real" artists), a few participate little or not at all, and most people are clustered in the undistinguished middle. It is like the speed of running: some people are very slow, some are amazingly fast, and the rest are in the middle. But the difference is that although all people would agree about how speed of running is distributed, and very few would be bothered by where they are in the distribution, most people do not believe that artistic creativity is normally distributed, and they regard their place in the distribution as a personal deficit. As I shall discuss in a later chapter, the issue is not the potential of everyone to be a great artist, but rather the personal and social consequences of the message that artistic creativity is a special gift of special people. It is a message that accepts the way things are, the way people appear to be. It is as clear a case of "blaming the victim" as one will find. It takes a Henry Schaefer-Simmern or a Kenneth Koch to challenge that message. Unfortunately, the hostess I discussed earlier did not see herself as a challenger of the conventional wisdom.

I turn now to an activity that only a few people regard as either artistic or creative. It is an example of how a narrow conception of artistic activity blinds one to its existence. I refer to the process of translating, be it a book from one language to another, or a novel for the theater or the movie screen. The case is most clear, both in an individual and a social sense, when the translation is from one language to another. The book appears with the words "translated by John Smith" in small print. To the reader, John Smith is someone somewhat above the level of a drudge who can use his or her knowledge of two languages to make a living. For most readers the translation is akin to the process of exchanging one currency for another. You have to know the equivalents, and if you run into a problem you can turn to a dictionary or other reference work for the answer. If John Smith's name appears in small print, it is because he is "only" an expert in two currencies. Indeed, I have heard people say that the day will come, sooner rather than later, when the computer will do the job of translation and, of course, with amazing speed.

I shared the conventional view until two decades ago when I read two of Edith Hamilton's books (1930, 1964) in which she discusses two related points: the degree to which American (and other) readers dislike reading Aeschylus, Sophocles, Aristophanes, and Euripides, and the role of the different translations of these Greek playwrights in engendering such dislike—in other words, why reading them is so frequently the opposite of *an experience*. She presents to the reader the different ways that different translators have handled particular passages. These translations vary markedly in readability, rhythm, and intelligibility. Some are far more literal than others. None of them met Miss Hamilton's criterion that a translation should make understandable to the American mind the imagery and force of the Greek mind of the time. She then proceeds to show how she would translate the passages. (Miss Hamilton at age ninety-two was not made a citizen of Athens in a public ceremony in that city for nothing!)

When I read her translation it was as if the clouds had parted and the sun came out. The words flowed, the imagery emerged clearly and forcefully, you wanted to read on and on, it was an experience. As best I, not being an expert, could gather, Miss Hamilton was not doing violence to the writings of these Greek playwrights, that is, putting them into an American English at the expense of their substance, imagery, message, and style. Far from catering to popular taste through inexcusable bowdlerization in an effort to serve pap to the millions, she made the minds of these ancients—in all their subtlety—intelligible and compelling.

The artist seeks to give overt expression to imagery within him- or herself. The struggle inheres in taming the chosen medium (language, color, wood, stone, sound, stage, movie screen) to one's imagery. It is a struggle. In the case of the translator, the struggle is complicated by the fact that two imageries in two different languages are involved. How do you go, so to speak, from imagery embedded in one foreign language *and* culture (past or present) to that embedded in another without distortion? How do you remain true to the author? The translator is like an actor trying to understand and convey his or her role in a play, to "read" or to intuit from the author's lines the psychological complexity of a role, and to convey that complexity, to make it believable to an audience. No one has described the translation process of the actor (and therefore of the translator) better than Constantin Stanislavski in *An Actor Prepares.* He points out that the task of the actor is to comprehend not only his or her role but also the relationships among roles in the drama. The playwright presents us with a slice or sample in time of an encapsulated culture, and the actor has to understand all those in that sample of relationships. Similarly, the translator has to comprehend not only a foreign language but the culture that language reflects, that is, the cultural nuances contained in words and phrases. But the translator has the added, extraordinarily difficult and creative task of conveying all this in a second language in a way that is true to the author's intent.[1]

The point here is not that translation, like acting, can be good, bad, or indifferent, and how to account for the variation. What I am calling attention to is that the process of translation is in every respect an artistic one, almost independent of variation among translators. (I say "almost" because there are instances when one has to conclude that the translation was literally mindless.) And in emphasizing the artistic nature of the translation process, I am calling attention to a cultural phenomenon: the narrow view of artistic activity, a view that scandalously underappreciates, if it does not totally ignore, superb manifestations of artistic activity. Translators will agree with me, and so will literary critics who have had to wade through translations that added to the archives labeled "snatching confusion from the jaws of clarity." But leaving all this aside, when you read a book on the title page of which (in small print) are the words "translated by John Smith," it says a good deal about the scope of our understanding of artistic activity and of how

---

1. Cynthia Ozick gives a concrete example of this process in an excellent article entitled "The Translator Becoming the Poet," in *Moment* 15, no. 1 (Feb. 1990): 50–53.

oversocialization into the culture puts blinders on us. It reveals not only what we are told to consider as artistic activity but also the scale of values by which we should judge such activity. We cannot escape making aesthetic judgments, but when they obscure or ignore the existence of the artistic process, they contribute mightily to the underestimation of artistic activity as a human attribute.

I have used the process of translation as an instance of underappreciation of the artistic process by the general public as well as by most of those who by conventional criteria are regarded as artists. Let me pursue the theme of underappreciation by turning to an activity that, I assume, no one would deny is quintessentially artistic in nature. I refer to the composing of music, more specifically, music composed for films. Two facts: I have never read a serious review of a film that mentioned its music, and I have never discussed a movie with anyone who in any way indicated that the music played a role in his or her appreciation, positive or negative, of the movie. And yet, if films were unaccompanied by music, is there any doubt that our affective response to, and even our understanding of, the film would be dramatically different? (Many readers will be too young to have been able to see films in the pre-talkies theater in which a piano player was up front adjusting the music to the requirements of the story. *Then* you were aware of the role of music!) The point is not that we are unaware of the role of music while we are watching the film, but rather that when we analyze our reactions and pass judgment on its artistic worth, the music is ignored. We say that the story was gripping or unconvincing, or the acting was good or bad, or the photography was stunning or unimpressive, and so on. Our words point to aspects that explain our reactions to ourselves and others. And we never note the music (musicals excepted). If that is true for an unsophisticated audience, it is only slightly less so in the case of the serious critic.

If no one doubts that composing music for films is an artistic process, its underappreciation is a reflection of a judgment (as in the case of translation) that the quality or complexity of the process is on the low side. This judgment says nothing at all about whether the music has its intended affective consequences but rather that the process qua process lacks the creativity and complexity of "serious" music; that is, it is like comparing apples and oranges. The fact is, of course, that in terms of growth processes apples and oranges share more commonalities than differences, and for the purpose of comprehending those growth processes their appearance and taste are relatively unimportant. It is one thing to say that "serious" music and music for film differ in numerous ways, but it is another thing to say that the processes that undergird their creation are different. In regard to any one of their differences, the variations within each of the two types is large and the overlap between the two is also large. "Serious" music is not all of a piece and neither is film music.

I have talked to translators. I have never had the opportunity to talk with composers of film music. Preparatory to talking with musicians I have tried to imagine what is involved in composing music for a movie. (The reader should try that exercise.) The more I thought about it the more completely artistic the process became. When I discussed this with "serious" musicians their initial response was similar, usually identical, to that of people to the process of translation. Yes, it is an artistic process but, please, let us not overestimate *that*. Two of these musicians asked: "Are you suggesting that a composer of music for a film is in the same league as Stravinsky or Tchaikovsky composing for a ballet?" My answer was in two parts. From the standpoint of impact on an audience and its aesthetic experience, they were in different leagues, although let us not forget that there are many ballets for which serious composers wrote undistinguished scores (just as there are films for which the music is distinguished). From the standpoint of artistic process, they were in the same league. Grandma Moses is not Degas, Schaefer-Simmern's students are not Matisse or (better yet) Rousseau. Koch's geriatric poets are not Whitman or Dickinson (or Koch). But in terms of the artistic process—its steps, problems, struggles, goals, and personal significances—they are more similar than different.

I have stressed the underappreciation of translation and composing for films because it is a derivative of the more general tendency to define the artistic process in a way that obscures its universality. It is not only that we define it in a most narrow way but, fatefully, that the definition carries with it judgments of worthiness that, accepted as they are generally, cause people to regard themselves as lacking whatever features the definition contains. The end result is a cultural self-fulfilling prophecy. To the extent that the definition divides the world in two—those who have it and those who do not—and to the extent that the culture supports that definition, assumption is confused with fact, what is with what can be, custom with what is "natural."

Far more often than not, we use the word *art* to refer to a product, an end result of a process. That use would not be problematic if it did not carry with it culturally determined meanings and judgments that restrict our understanding of the process by which works of art are created, a restriction that leads us to ignore its existence and/or to offer explanations that are illogical and obfuscating. Let me illustrate this point by an example outside the arena of artistic activity. Imagine that your neighbor's child has taken your cat and choked it to death. And assume that the child has an IQ of 180. You would say that the child is "sick," that the act is incomprehensible apart from a preceding series of thoughts, feelings, fantasies, and psychological mechanisms. You would *not* say that the murderous act was *caused* by the high IQ. What are you likely to say if your neighbor's child has an IQ of 50? That the act is explained by the low IQ. In the one instance we ignore process, we offer the grossest oversimplification, even though a part of us knows that among all those with an IQ of 50 such a murderous act is indeed rare. That two children with wildly different IQs can, in terms of process, have similar processes in common does not occur to us. Because one child is labeled "bright" and the other "dumb" or "mentally retarded," we are culturally schooled to ignore their commonalities. Our labels and definitions tell us about differences, not similarities. That is their legitimate purpose, but when they cause us to be insensitive to commonalities in process and, fatefully, to regard, treat, and explain people in unjustifiably and illogically different ways, they are more destructive than they are useful.

So, mentally retarded individuals are not supposed to have a creative spark, or to engage in artistic activity until someone like Schaefer-Simmern comes along with the assumption of artistic activity as a universal human attribute, and with a conception of how it can be nurtured and developed, and then we are forced to pay attention to process. And when we see what he and others have enabled "ordinary people" to accomplish through artistic activity, it should lead us to reexamine questions like what is art? who is an artist? what is the artistic process? on what basis do we make good judgments of artistic worthiness? These are not narrow questions. They concern not only our conception of human potential, but how that conception is embedded in and reinforces our culture and social order. Therein lies its challenge to psychology.

Most people regard themselves as the opposite of artistic. That kind of self-regard is hard to shake in people even when you present them with evidence that they do engage in the artistic process: that is, by using color, form, diverse materials, and media to organize, to order, to externalize internal imagery in a way that is satisfying to them because it is *theirs*. They may be dissatisfied with the product and seek to change it so that it better fits their internal conception. There are times when the process of changing goes on indefinitely: the person is never satisfied, she thinks she can do better according to her criteria. As good an example as any is gardening. I have known people for whom gardening is a passion. For them, gardening is not planning, fertilizing, pruning, or producing a mass of engaging colors. They have a picture of what they would like to create, taking into account topography, the kinds of plants, or bushes, or trees they prefer, climate and seasonal distribution of sunlight. It is an internal picture, complex both in organization and in process of execution. It is a picture that is truly unique, it is *theirs*, and the struggle inheres in translating that picture into an external reality. *They* know what *they* want to *see*, and their satisfaction is in the process and the seeing. Whether the garden is small or large is irrelevant.

There are professionals whom we call (or who call themselves) landscape artists. Most people would hesitate to call the gardeners artists—another example of how labels obscure commonalities of process. It is not surprising that the gardeners I have known and interviewed do not regard themselves as artists. It is as if as a group they are saying: "How can the likes of us be regarded as the likes of artists?" They confuse the scale of effort and even the quality or "success" of the end product with the process they employed. When I challenged one of these gardeners, who was very knowledgeable in the visual arts, she thought for a while and then said: "Every great artist has at one time or another been dissatisfied with his or her efforts, but we don't say that they were not engaged in the artistic process." It was this woman who said that if my position meant that she was an artist in the same sense as Frederick Olmstead (the great landscape architect who, among scores of other things, created Central Park and Prospect Park in New York City), she would have to disagree.

Of the different aspects of artistic activity, none is more obvious and pervasive in the process than the sense of psychological ownership: that what one seeks to create "out there" is in accord with an internal picture and conception. If we concentrate only on the end product, rendering our inevitable judgments to what we see, we contribute to insensitivity to the artistic process—that is, we overlook the existence of the process, especially if our standards derive from knowledge of what tradition has stamped as "great" art. So, when you look at the productions of Schaefer-Simmern's mentally retarded, institutionalized students in terms of your reactions to Van Gogh paintings, the differences are obvious, so obvious that you may find it impossible to believe that they are both end products of similar processes. You might find it more believable if you could have observed the energy that accompanied the struggles of these students to externalize *their* internal conceptions. And if you had observed the peers of these students in the industrial training program mindlessly making rugs, baskets, and chairs according to procedures laid down by their teachers, you would see the difference between artistic creativity and assembly-line routine. The experiential and conceptual gulf between them and Schaefer-Simmern's students is infinitely greater than that between his students and Van Gogh. His students created and psychologically "owned" (literally and figuratively) their products; their peers did not.

When he ended his stay at the Southbury Training School to go to the University of California at Berkeley, Schaefer-Simmern was plagued by feelings of guilt because he knew that the students whose self-regard he had dramatically altered and whose artistic development was similarly dramatic would be returning to a stultifying institutional routine. Their days of psychological ownership of an activity were over. I have to assume that this was also what happened to Koch's students in the ghetto elementary school and the nursing home.

When I asserted that artistic activity is a universal human attribute, I was implying that it is an activity, a process, that gains much of its force and satisfaction from the sense that what is being created, the end product, would to some degree be isomorphic with an internal conception expressive of the creator, a product unique to the creator. It is that need for psychological ownership that never gets truly extinguished, although most people have "learned" that they are *unable* to give ordered expression to that need; that whatever else they are, they are not artists. And when, as in the case of the gardener I interviewed, they do engage in an artistic activity that results in something they "own," they humbly decline being put in the category of artist. They confuse process with the value they put on the product. More correctly, they put a value on the product that they think others will. Process is ignored or irrelevant. Unfortunately, however, most people never get to the point where they engage in the artistic process and can disagree with someone's opinion about them as artists.

If most people come to regard artistic activity as alien to their capabilities, it is in part because we have been taught that there is "great art," not-so-great art, and art that really does not deserve to be called art. Of course there are or should be ways by which we place different values on different works of art. In making these distinctions, what is unfortunate is that they rivet our attention on the end products of the artistic activity and cause us to ignore the activity itself; we illogically and unwarrantedly conclude that two end products that are obviously different in appearance and in what they elicit from us are the results of two very or totally different processes. This is what John Dewey in 1896 called the psychological or historical fallacy: "A set of considerations which hold good only because of a completed process, is read into the content of the process which conditions this completed result. A state of things characterizing an outcome is regarded as a true description of the events which led up to this outcome; when, as a matter of fact, if this outcome had already been in existence, there would have been no necessity for the process" (Dewey, 1963, p. 262). If two works of art differ, and dramatically so, it does not follow that the "necessity" to create those works and the processes from which they emerge have nothing in common. It is one thing to view a great work of art and to conclude that you cannot do something comparable in value; it is quite another thing to conclude that you are incapable of engaging in artistic activity. But that is precisely what most people are taught to conclude.

I have been emphasizing the untoward consequences of ignoring or being insensitive to the artistic process. It is not only that we fail to note that process where it exists, but also that as aesthetic responders our appreciation of the end products is superficial—we usually respond to the work of art that we see without seeking to comprehend the process that gave rise to it. For example, when we see a stage play or film that bores us, we usually do not attempt to fathom what in the artistic process contributed to our judgment. We might say that the story was silly or was without dramatic impact, or the acting was poor. We are not likely to deny that what we saw was the result of an artistic process, although in rendering our negative judgment we imply that the process was somehow faulty. But how do we respond when we meet someone who was stirred by the play or film, who thought it was just terrific? The conversation usually terminates in agreement that there is no accounting for taste, or that one reaction is "right" and the other "wrong." Passing judgment on what we literally see is inevitable, but that level of appreciation should not blind us to the artistic process qua process. I am sure there are readers who will have responded to the work of Koch's and Schaefer-Simmern's students in a ho-hum, impassive way, quite in contrast to the way in which Koch or Schaefer-Simmern (or John Dewey) was stirred. The difference, of course, is that they were responding as much to the process as to the end products. I am not suggesting that liking or not liking a work of art is unimportant or to be eschewed, but rather that such judgments, precisely because we have been socialized to remain at that level of judgment, restrict our recognition of the nature and existence of artistic activity.

These thoughts were engendered by my reading *A Life,* the auto-biography of Elia Kazan (1988), who directed some stirring and com-pelling stage plays and films in the post–World War II period. It is a fascinating book on many scores, but several are relevant to my pur-poses. I saw many of his productions, and to say that I "liked" them is to indulge in understatement. The fact is that what I liked is what I saw and experienced. The stories gripped me, the acting was superb, seeing each production was *an experience.* I knew that Kazan had been the director but I had no understanding of what that meant. He played no part in *my* experience. It was not only that I was ignorant of the direc-torial process, his artistic process, but that I was not interested in the process. What I find so fascinating in his book is the way he describes and illuminates the directorial, artistic process. He does this with a clarity that deepened my understanding of where and how things can go awry in that process. I can no longer see a play or a film, regardless of whether I respond positively or negatively, without trying to under-stand the relationship between appearance and process. The tendency to be insensitive to process, even when we know that what we have seen is a work of art, makes it all too easy to overlook the presence of artistic activity in what we have been taught to regard as works of non-art. In scientific research we are made sensitive to the possibility of "false negatives"—concluding that some phenomenon is not true or does not exist when in fact it does, or that a person does not possess certain characteristics when in fact he or she does. Awareness of that kind of possibility is precisely what powered Schaefer-Simmern and Koch to do what they did.

There is a difference between what we ordinarily mean by "appre-ciating" a work of art and "respecting" it. In the former use we usually restrict ourselves to liking or not liking the work of art; in the latter we try to fathom the nature and problems of the artistic process. We may not like the poetry of Koch's students, but that does not excuse our failing to comprehend their artistic process.

Another reason I found Kazan's autobiography so instructive and interesting has to do with one of the crucial ingredients of the artistic process: the sense of "psychological ownership," the sense that the end product you seek to create is uniquely yours. It is not a compromise between what you seek to create and what others require of you. It is the opposite of imitation; it is *yours*. What is created may be viewed by others as derivative or not, as interesting or not, but to the creator the work bears his or her unique imprint, it is the realization in a palpable, visual way of an internal visual conception the person struggled to create. Relatively late in his career Kazan came to the conclusion that he no longer wanted to direct plays and films. He no longer wanted to work with and through playwrights, actors, producers, scenic designers, and those whose financial role gave them (or who thought it gave them) a voice in matters artistic. For Kazan, the end product was never wholly his. This is not to say that he devalued what he had done but rather that with one or two exceptions the end product was a compromise between his conceptions and those of others. As he indicates, he put his stamp on each of his productions, but it was to him a *faint stamp*, one that was not wholly Kazan. That feeling festered and grew stronger over time until he decided that in whatever he was going to do *he* had to determine *by himself* the shape of his artistic work. He began to write novels. At last there was no one mediating between what he wanted to say and what the world would hear.

Kazan is not, of course, the first artist to un-imprison himself or herself from a particular style or medium or cultural pressure. Indeed, formally trained artists honor those who over the centuries successfully went against the mainstream, where creativity and need for psychological ownership changed the history of the field. Mature artists like Kazan—those who have, so to speak, paid their dues in the club of artists—can make these dramatic moves. But what about young children whose artistry and delight in ownership get prematurely stifled by the pressure to make their works meet the predetermined criteria of adults? In their own way these adults paid their dues, but to a club whose rules, regulations, and traditions were antithetical to and not supportive of the artistic process. And what about the millions of "non-artists" who are quite aware of their fantasies of creativity and ownership, but are unwilling and unable to challenge their status of "non-artist" and self-select themselves for the club of "pedestrian minds"? What I find truly remarkable is how many members of this club engage in artistic activity, although they and the world do not see it as such.

I am reminded here how, until the latter part of the nineteenth century, what today we call African art was for all practical purposes considered non-art. Like children's art, it simply was not taken seriously. That these strange-appearing works were end products of a complicated artistic process, owned by the creators no less than by the culture around them, was a possibility that could not be entertained. The creators of these works (which ranged from the simple to the very complex) were seen through a lens distorted by such labels as primitive, barbaric, and unrealistic. How could people like that engage in the traditionally conceived artistic process? How could Schaefer-Simmern's mentally retarded students, as well as his "ordinary people," be considered artists? How could Koch's elementary school children and his nursing home students be expected to engage in artistic activity?

Worldviews are undergirded by axioms that by their very nature are so "right, natural, and proper" that they do not have to be verbalized. They are taken for granted and go unchallenged. Two examples. Someone asks you this question: when you review everything you thought or did today, what unverbalized axiom were you accepting as true which, if it were not true, would make what you thought or did today incomprehensible? That axiom is that you will be alive tomorrow. We know we are mortal, but our lives are based on an axiom of immortality. Cultures differ markedly in this respect. The second example is less upsetting, but its acceptance in our society has come to have serious consequences. It is that education should take place in encapsulated classrooms in encapsulated schools. In my book *Schooling in America,* I examine and reject the validity of that axiom, and I conclude that as long as we continue to accept it the goal of improving education cannot be achieved. Whether or not you agree with my argument and conclusion is not relevant here. I mention it only to make the point that our worldview of education rests on, among other things, a particular axiom we never have to verbalize because our socialization into our society has been so successful in putting that axiom into our psychological bloodstream. Few things are more potent than axioms in short-circuiting challenges to accustomed thought, practice, and institutional existence. And for a good reason: verbalizing and examining axioms can be, usually are, upsetting to the individual and the social order because they alert you to a new universe of alternatives.

An axiom that undergirds our worldview of artistic activity states that a few people have a lot of artistic talent, somewhat more people have less talent, but most people have none at all. I am by no means the first to challenge that axiom, nor am I the first to argue that if that axiom is invalid, in whole or in part, we must reexamine not only our psychological theories but the nature of our society as well. What we call a worldview (and every culture, past or present, has a distinctive worldview) always contains a conception of the nature of human nature, the goals of living, and ways in which social living should be organized. Worldviews have the function of insuring continuity and stability, and, therefore, when a worldview is challenged the predictable response is rejection because, like a work of art, when you change one feature of it, you quickly find that you have to change other features also. Over the millenia, worldviews have changed, but never quickly and without turmoil.

In this and the previous chapters I have been concerned only with the narrowness of our conception of the artistic process and its consequences for how people come to regard themselves. I have not attempted a definition or analysis of the process which has developmental, familial, cultural, and educational aspects and manifests itself in myriad ways with diverse media. I have pointed to certain ingredients of that process, not for the purposes of definition, but to indicate how our customary view of it obscures us to its existence. Nor has my discussion in any way been undergirded by the mistaken belief that everyone has the potential to be a great or good artist—that is, to be regarded as such by others. Such a belief confuses the process with judgments of worth. What I do believe is that the unwarranted acceptance of the axiom robs people of the satisfaction that is so frequently a consequence of engaging in the process. It is a satisfaction that comes not from indulgence but from a willing struggle to put one's imprint on a configured, externalized piece of work. It is a satisfaction that propels one to stay with the process, to experience change and the sense of growth. That we may not like or value the product is less important (for my present purposes) than the process and its significance for the producer, now and for the future.

The degree to which we nurture an activity depends in large part on our conception of the nature of that activity. As I have indicated in regard to artistic activity, we are taught about its nature in subtle and blatant ways that not only prevent most people from engaging in the activity but also render them incompetent to appreciate works of art.

In the next chapter I will turn to the messages people are sent about how they should respond to works of art. Those messages, like television commercials, are intended to shape our thinking, values, and behavior. They are windows on the nature of our society.

8 ◆ INTIMIDATION AND LEARNED HELPLESSNESS

The creation of and response to a work of art—or the failure to note and respond to a work of art—are never neutral affairs; they are always in some way a manifestation of a culture. The artistic process is a kind of constant regardless of culture, however much it may vary in terms of the substance, form, and meanings of the products to which it gives rise. It is almost always the case that the artist intends that others will respond to his or her work—that they will note and appreciate it. And it is almost always the case that the artist titles the work, thereby suggesting to the viewer or reader some aspect of its meaning for its creator. The title is a message, testimony to the social nature of the activity. In non-Western cultures, present and past, titles are often unnecessary because artist and community agree on the meaning and social function of the work. This is not to say that the work does not have significances for the artist apart from the shared agreement. It is to say that the viewer has no doubt about what the artist intended the viewer to understand and appreciate. And, frequently, in these societies the viewing public knows the artist and has observed the artist at work.

In Western societies it was long the case, especially in religious art, that titles were unnecessary, again because their meanings and functions were obvious. Michelangelo's *Pietà* did not really need a title for the viewing public to understand its content and function. But in the past several centuries that degree of shared understanding has dramatically decreased. At the same time that an artist displays his or her work, testifying to the goal of influencing or impacting upon the viewer, some artists will proclaim indifference to and even rejection of the viewer's expectations; they see themselves as apart from a larger community. And some refuse to assign titles to their works as if to say that the process of creation and the meanings of the work for the artist should be matters of indifference to the viewer.

Titled or not, a work of art is intended to be appreciated, to engender in the viewer *an* experience. And by appreciation the artist, certainly the art critic, means more than superficial expressions of like or dislike. Many writers maintain that the process of appreciation is or should be creative in that the viewer uses his or her own knowledge and experience to understand the sources of liking and disliking. That is to say, the viewer no less than the artist starts with an internal vision or conception or reaction, which then leads to a process of analysis and reanalysis, of relating one aspect to another, culminating in an understanding that is far more complicated than liking or disliking. Liking and disliking are starting points that at the end of the viewing process are embedded in a new understanding of the picture, novel, poem, play, film, and so on. From this perspective the viewer adopts the opposite of a passive stance, unafraid to pursue the process of creating what for the viewer is a new and enriched understanding. In terms of liking or disliking, the viewer may end up where he or she started, but only in a linguistic sense is that initial reaction the same; that is, liking or disliking are now in a different psychological context. If the creation of a work of art involves struggle, so does or should the process of viewing. Art is more than what we conventionally mean by entertainment.

These expectations rest on several judgments. The first, of course, is that a work of art is intended to stimulate feeling *and* thought. It is not intended to be regarded fleetingly or superficially. The second is that as viewers we should feel obliged to go beyond our initial affective response in order to understand what it is about the work "out there" that contributed to our reaction. We should accord respect to what the artist has done, at least to the point where we comprehend how the work transacted with our knowledge and experience. The third judgment, implied in the second, is that creative viewing is an unrivaled source of personal, intellectual, and educational satisfaction and enrichment: something within us gets changed, added to, transformed. It can and should be an experience. The fourth judgment is usually the most explicit and unchallenged: works of art are instances of man's unique creativity, aspirations, and enduring accomplishments. Art is what sets the human organism apart from all other forms of life. To create works of art is distinctively human. It is an activity that we should respect and treasure. Therefore, viewing such works is a serious affair.

These are great expectations. Why, then, are they unrealized in most people? Why do so many people live their lives without viewing or even noting works of art? Why in the case of film, the most popular art form, is appreciation usually limited to expressions of like and dislike? Let us start with the most frequent reaction to a work of art. Indeed, it is a ubiquitous response. I refer to the fact that in one way or another we *respond*. We cannot control responding immediately. That immediate response may be vague, global, specific, compelling; a rejection or a puzzlement. But respond we do, and that is as true for the sophisticated critic as for all others. To deny the existence of that immediate response, to say that it should be avoided, is as realistic as trying to stop the ocean tides.[1] Far from giving such counsel, one can look at it as a beginning engagement, a spontaneous expression of interest. Just as we have come to see the scribbles of young children as an inevitable beginning phase in the development of the artistic process, so should we regard reactions of like and dislike. The scribbles of children may not move us at all, but we do not (at least should not) try to dissuade the child from the activity because we should know that this is what the child is capable of at that point.

If the parent knows this, he or she may encourage the child to stay with the activity and may be alert to indications that the child is moving out of that phase of artistic activity. If, as is usually the case, the parent views scribbles as *just* scribbles, as a kind of end rather than a starting point, as a developmentally meaningless or unimportant activity requiring no special attention, it is likely that the value the child will

---

1. This point is in all respects identical to how we react to another person. In his pathbreaking study "Forming Impressions of Personality," S. E. Asch (1946) begins by saying: "We look at a person and immediately a certain impression of his character forms itself in us. A glance, a few spoken words are sufficient to tell us a story about a highly complex matter. . . . Subsequent observation may enrich or upset our first view, but we can no more prevent its rapid growth than we can avoid perceiving a given visual object or hearing a melody" (p. 258). Asch concludes: "that forming an impression is an organized process; that characteristics are perceived in their dynamic relations; that central qualities are discovered, leading to the distinction between them and peripheral qualities; that relations of harmony and contradiction are observed" (p. 283).

The immediate response, be it to a person or work of art, is or can be a starting point for a more enriched understanding of structure *and* self only if people are disposed or are required to go beyond that immediate response. In regard to works of art, that disposition or inclination has been effectively aborted in most people; daily living makes it more likely that forming an impression of people will go beyond the immediate reaction. To ignore or devalue the immediate response of an individual to a work of art is by any educational psychology inexcusable.

accord the activity is the same as that of the parent. The point of danger arises when the child goes beyond scribbles. It is then that most parents will seek to teach the child to make his or her products "realistic"; cultural values take precedence over both the child's capacities and his or her likes and dislikes. The most frequent and fateful consequence is that the child no longer wishes to engage in the activity.

In regard to the appreciation of art, the responses of liking and disliking have early origins. Although it is hard to overestimate the influence on children of adult judgments about how realistic or representational an artistic product should be, it would be wrong to assume that the child's likes and dislikes are identical with those of adults. And that is the point: the child keeps his judgments silent. He or she is rendered incompetent in terms of both the artistic process and its products. Of course, this is not what parents intend. If they do not understand what is at stake, they should not be scapegoated. This lack of understanding has to be seen as an expression of two things basic in the culture: a narrow conception of human abilities and the assimilation of values that say, so to speak, that this ability is more important than that ability—that some universal cognitive accomplishments are more worthy than others. Artistic activity is clearly low on that scale of values (if not off of it, for most people).

Let me give two examples. Parents expect that their newborn will learn to talk, and many parents will respond to any indication that the child is going beyond babbles (=scribbles) and is making sounds that smack of words. The parents respond not only with glee but with action that support and reinforce what they assume to be a developmental milestone; that is, they know that in some way there is a developmental sequence to which they should pay attention. Far from being indifferent to babblings and what they think of as approximations to words, they treasure the activity. And the earlier the child seems to be moving to articulated words, the more delighted parents are about this seeming precocity.

The developmental sequence by which the child goes from babbles to rudimentary phrases and sentences is complicated but predictable. Throughout the sequence the parent accepts, up to a point, whatever sounds the child makes. At some point the parent begins to try to shape those sounds in an effort to teach the child "real" language. What tends to go unnoticed and has not been studied is the frequency with which the child responds with obvious anger to the parental effort. It is as if the child does not understand the parent's effort, as if what the parent articulates or points to is not what the child intended. I have observed this in the case of parents so pathetically eager to demonstrate the child's "intelligence" that they are unaware that they are setting goals for their child at variance with the child's intentions and cognitive level. I have also observed parents who are so indifferent to or ignorant of the sequence as to produce "delayed speech" in their child. Although these observations are the exceptions, I note them in order to indicate that, as in the case of children's artistic endeavors, the attempt to influence the child to articulate sounds that are "real" can be a source of difficulty, for the child at least.

These untoward effects aside—and I do not want to exaggerate the frequency and consequences of the child's difficulty—parents attach a degree of importance to the articulation of language that simply is not the case for artistic activity. I am, of course, not suggesting that the two activities should have the same importance, although I would argue that from a life-span perspective the failure to engage in artistic activity, in some way at some level, impoverishes living. I assume that people who lack speech would prefer to be otherwise, however well they develop a substitute for their disability. I also assume that those who go through life regarding themselves as lacking in creativity and incapable of engaging in some form of artistic activity also wish that it were otherwise.

The second example is reading. Many parents assign the highest value to learning to read. They provide the preschooler with picture books, they read books to the child, and they make up stories that they hope will stimulate the preschooler to want to read. When television first became available, some parents did not purchase a set because of the possibility that viewing would overwhelm or become a poor substitute for reading. For a child to be uninterested in reading or to manifest some kind of handicap in learning to read engenders anxiety in parents. When the child does not take to reading, it is nightmarish for parents as they envision poor school performance and the inability to enter a good college. To say that in our culture learning to read is important is to state the obvious. Those parents whose children are readers before they start kindergarten are the envy of others. Reading is an activity that most parents treasure, encourage, and support, and they usually show it in ways appropriate to the child's interests and capacity.

It is, again, quite a different story in the case of artistic activity. Artistic activity in children is not highly valued. It would, perhaps, be more correct to say that in the culture generally the nurturing of artistic activity in children has no distinctive developmental value. Liking or disliking artistic activity or its products originates before formal schooling begins and becomes crystallized during the school years. Beginning in kindergarten, especially in kindergarten, the child is explicitly "taught" what is acceptable in his or her creations. Far more often than not, children are told what to draw or make and to judge those works according to criteria set by the teacher. From kindergarten through the higher grades children learn to regard art in the same way they regard the solution of an arithmetic problem or the date of a historical event: there is a right and a wrong answer, and the teacher knows the difference.

I am reminded here of Max Wertheimer's (1945) famous study of the way that children solve the parallelogram problem. When Wertheimer demonstrated to the children that there was more than one way of arriving at a proof, they categorically denied that these alternative ways were right because they conflicted with what they had been taught. How children are taught to regard their art products or those of others is no different. To expect children to like to engage in artistic activity, to "appreciate" art appreciation, is to expose one's ignorance of the modal classroom in the school culture. What would be mystifying is if children had more positive attitudes—that would really require explanation! If the spontaneous creative artistic activity of preschoolers is not in evidence during formal schooling, this says a good deal more about the school culture than about the interests and capabilities of children generally. As I have said before, with rare exceptions schools make no serious attempt to stimulate and guide artistic development. Today we hear much about "scientific illiteracy" and how schools must do a better job of making science as knowledge *and* process more interesting and relevant for students. We want students to like science, to see it as important for their intellectual development. Indeed, there are those who insist that students should begin in the earliest grades to engage in the scientific process at a level appropriate to their personal experience and cognitive level. And engaging means far more than acquiring important knowledge. This is no less the case with artistic activity. Let me illustrate what engagement should mean by the following quotation about conventional "science education":

What we mean by "physical-knowledge activities" can be best explained by contrasting these with activities typically found in "science education." For illustrative purposes we shall present two different ways of teaching an activity on crystals. The first, quoted from a text on preschool education, is an example of the "science education" approach:

Theme: Crystals

Behavioral Objective: At the end of the experience, the child will be able to:

1. Pick out crystals when shown a variety of things.
2. Define what a crystal is.
3. Discuss the steps in making crystals at school.

Learning Activities

The teacher will show the children different crystals and rocks. She will explain what a crystal is and what things are crystals (sand, sugar, salt, etc.). Then she will show some crystals she made previously. The children are given materials . . . so they can make crystals to take home. A magnifying glass is used so the children can examine the crystals.

Method 1: Mix ½ cup each of salt, bluing, water, and 1 T (tablespoon) ammonia. Pour over crumpled paper towels. In 1 hour crystals begin to form. They reach a peak in about 4 hours and last for a couple of days.

Maureen Ellis, one of our teacher colleagues, read the above lesson, modified it into a physical-knowledge activity, and wrote the following account of her teaching with crystals:

"While looking through an early-education texts, I found the "recipe" for making crystals. I decided to do it, but not as a science project because I had no idea why crystals formed. It was as much magic to me as to the kids; so we used it like a cooking activity. I told them that we didn't know why it happened, but they got the idea that when some things mix together, something extraordinary happens. The activity was such a success that for days individual children were showing others how to make crystals, and some made their "own" to take home.

"This experiment inspired other experiments and a whole atmosphere of experimentation. One boy, during cleanup, decided to pour the grease from the popcorn pan into a cup with water and food coloring. He put it on the windowsill until the next day. He was sure "something" would happen and was surprised when nothing much did. Another child said she knew an experiment with salt, soap and pepper (which she had seen on television). She demonstrated for those who were interested. A third child was inspired by the soap experiment to fill a cup with water and put a bar of soap in. She was astonished by the change in water level and then tested other things in the water—a pair of scissors, chalk, crayon, and her hand to see the change in water level.

"The next day, one child brought a cup filled with beans, blue water, styrofoam packing materials, and a Q-Tip. 'This is my experiment. Cook it,' he said. So I asked what he thought would happen to each of the things in the cup. He made a few predictions and I told him we could cook it the next day. (I wanted to experiment first to see if there might be anything dangerous involved.) At group time, he told everyone about his experiment, and the group made predictions which I wrote on the blackboard. Among these were: 'The whole thing will get hot,' 'the water will change color,' 'the beans will get cooked, and you can eat them,' and 'the beans will grow.' When I asked, 'Will anything melt?" the children said that the styrofoam would not melt but the Q-Tip would. The next day, the child did his cooking experiment, and wrote down the results with my help. Many of his predictions were found to be true, but there were some surprises. It smelled terrible, the Q-Tip did not melt, and the whole thing bubbled."

In the "science education" approach above, the teacher's objective is for the child to learn about crystals. More specifically the objectives are to get children to become able to recognize and define crystals, and to describe how they can be made. In this content-centered approach, children listen to explanations, look at what the teacher shows, and do what he or she planned.

In the "physical-knowledge" approach, by contrast, the teacher's objective is for children to pursue the problems and questions they come up with. The purpose of making crystals is thus not to teach about crystals per se, but to stimulate various ideas within a total atmosphere of experimentation. In the situation reported above, the making of crystals inspired four children in four different ways—to make "something" with grease from the popcorn pan, to make specks of pepper "swim" in water, to watch what happens to the water level when various objects are dropped into a container, and to cook a variety of objects. It also stimulated other children to think about many possible outcomes, and encouraged decentering through exchange of ideas about what might happen. The physical-knowledge approach thus emphasizes children's initiative, their actions on objects, and their observation of the feedback from objects.

All babies and young children are naturally interested in examining objects, acting on them, and observing the objects' reactions. Our aim in physical-knowledge activities is to use this spontaneous interest by encouraging children to structure their knowledge in ways that are natural extensions of the knowledge they already have. Thus, learning in the physical-knowledge approach is always rooted in the child's natural development.

As we saw in the lesson on crystals, "science education" basically unloads adult-organized content on children.[2]

The criticisms these authors make about conventional science education can be made of art education as well. No one more than Piaget has

2. Constance Kamii and R. D. De Vries, *Physical Knowledge in Preschool Education* (Englewood Cliffs, N.J.: Prentice-Hall, 1978), pp. 3–6.

studied and illuminated how scientific thinking develops and unfolds in children (in preschool and beyond), just as no one more than Schaefer-Simmern has done the same for the unfolding of artistic activity. Piaget wrote the preface to the Kamii and De Vries book, to my knowledge the only time he agreed to do that for a book on pedagogy. His reluctance is alluded to in the first sentence of his preface, a part of which follows:

> Many educators have used our operatory tasks by transforming them into kinds of standardized "tests," as if their purposes were to diagnose the performances a child is capable of in a given situation. Our method of asking questions with free conversations, as well as the theory of the formation of structures which we have studied stage by stage, permit a much more nuanced use of these tasks—to know how a child reasons and what kinds of new constructions he is capable of when we encourage his spontaneity to a maximum. In this case the double advantage which can be obtained is: (1) from the standpoint of psychological diagnosis, to foresee in part the progress the child will be able to make later; and (2) from the pedagogical point of view, to reinforce his constructivity and thus find a method of teaching in accordance with "constructivism" which is the fundamental principle of our interpretation of intellectual development.
>
> This is what the authors of this book have well understood. I had already visited with great pleasure in 1967 the Ypsilanti Public Schools (Michigan) and observed the efforts made there to develop the pupils' creativity. The new experiments done by the authors at the University of Illinois at Chicago Circle are inspired by the same principles: Focusing on physical knowledge more than on logico-mathematical knowledge, they centered their effort on inventing activities to permit children to act on objects and observe the reactions or transformations of these objects (which is the essence of physical knowledge, where the role of the subject's actions is indispensable for understanding the nature of the phenomena involved). (P. vii)

For Piaget and Schaefer-Simmern engagement is a constructive process: acting on and in turn being acted on, an ongoing transformation between "in there" and "out there," a willing pursuit powered by curiosity, interest, and the desire to master. It is knowledge acquired by action, not passive receptivity, knowledge about self and the world, and what that self can *effect*.

As I have argued in *Schooling in America,* the hope that science education will be improved will not, indeed cannot, be realized until there is a radical change not only in how schools are structured but in how seriously we take the notion of active engagement. But I have not brought science education into this discussion to make that point but rather to indicate that if students do not like science, or regard themselves as scientifically inept, or conclude that science is incomprehensible to their "ordinary" minds, the explanation is not all that obscure. If students do not take to science, it is for the same reasons that some do not take to art. The difference is that as a society we say that we need science and scientists, and *need* is too weak a word to express the value we place on both. In that sense ours is obviously not a society that says it needs art and artists. And yet, the sources of scientific illiteracy—worse yet, student dislike of the teaching of science—are precisely those that account for artistic illiteracy.

By the end of formal schooling (including college), young adults have one or all of several attitudes about art. The most frequent is that art is what you see in museums or galleries and are expected to respect and like. They know, of course, that some art and artists are not represented in museums, and that that says something about their quality. There is "great art" and "not-so-great art." They know the names of the "great" artists and may even be able to match one or two of their works with their names. (Indeed, because of movies and television they probably know the names of more great artists than of great scientists.) They rarely visit museums except on those occasions (museum directors call them "happenings") when a well-publicized exhibit of a "master" has been mounted. They go more out of respect, duty, a desire to absorb "culture," or sheer curiosity than because they seek or expect an experience. And at these happenings they find themselves in a quandary because they do not like all the works equally, and yet they feel they should because all are the works of an incontestible, socially acclaimed master. With earphones attached to an audio cassette, they stand in front of a painting listening to a voice telling them why the work is notable, why they should like it; at the same time they are puzzled at their own lack of affective response. The do seek to comprehend more than what strikes the eye, they want to have an experience, but more often than not they obey the voice that tells them to move on to the next work.

The point I wish to emphasize is the sincerity of the desire to understand, so to speak, what the shouting is all about, why they like this work and not that one, what it is they are missing, what they lack that prevents them from appreciating what they have been told they should appreciate. Their viewing starts and ends with the belief that there is a right way and a wrong way of experiencing art, and clearly they do not know the right way. They find themselves in a position similar to that of the child plaguing him- or herself with questions about how babies are created and born, posing these questions inchoately or otherwise to adults, and getting no satisfactory answers. Unlike the child who answers the questions in his or her own private, fantastic way, most viewers of art never know how to answer their questions except by concluding that they are incompetent. They blame themselves, a conclusion they arrived at—they were taught to arrive at—long before they set foot in a museum. The artistic process is alien territory, an activity with which they cannot identify. It is psychologically foreign to their experience, and when faced with the products of the process, they can only respond with liking, disliking, or puzzlement.

It is one thing to regret such reactions, it is quite another thing to derogate them as expressions of philistinism, another instance of blaming the victim. But what is most unfortunate is that most people cannot verbalize their reactions because they fear criticism or derision, just as they previously feared the reactions of adults to their artistic efforts, spontaneous or required. I am reminded here of what I observed watching Schaefer-Simmern with his mentally retarded pupils and his "ordinary" adults. With both kinds of groups his initial and most difficult task was helping the participants overcome their fear that what they had done was wrong or unworthy. When they finished a work and showed it to Schaefer-Simmern, their facial expressions reflected the anticipation of criticism, often accompanied by self-derogatory phrases. Their obvious stance was: "Who am I to create something worthy of anyone's attention and respect?" I expected this stance in the institutionalized retarded individuals whose entire lives reinforced the self-derogatory stance. The "ordinary" people had even more difficulty accepting the possibility that they were capable of creating an ordered expression of an internal vision or conception. These were educated people who knew about art in a conventional way and who from time to time had gone to exhibits. The group I observed most systematically was comprised of institutional staff who, having observed Schaefer's work with the retarded residents, requested that he form a small group of staff members. And yet, although they were a self-selected group, highly motivated, their "fear and trembling" when they displayed their initial efforts were obvious. And those reactions were accompanied by self-derogatory comments—"Obviously, I am not an artist," "I know this is terrible," "If you laugh at what I have done, I'll understand."

Despite Schaefer-Simmern's reassurances, his caution that it was impossible to imitate nature or reality, and his exhortation to draw what they could see clearly in their minds' eye (however simple that might appear), only two of the six in the group experienced an unfolding or development of their artistic activity. The others gave up in despair, convinced that they lacked even a dim spark of creativity. They started with the judgment that what they did should look like what reality said it should look like, and they ended up even more convinced that that judgment was valid. In Schaefer-Simmern's terms, they were "spoiled" by a lifetime of experience that not only confused process with product but also instilled in them what a product should look like. Artistic activity is never an individual affair. As activity and attitude it is suffused with cultural definitions and expectations.

I have emphasized the point that we have no control over our response to a work of art. We are expected to respond and we do. We find ourselves liking or disliking what is before us, or puzzled by our lack of responsive engagement. The problem that arises for most people is whether their liking or disliking is for the "right" reasons. In some vague way they believe—they have been taught to believe—that it is not sufficient to remain at the level of liking or disliking, that to appreciate a work of art requires an analysis of which features of the work elicited their response. They have also been told that a work of art should be understood (can be understood) only in terms of when the artist lived (or is living), the influences on the artist, and the conventions to which he adapted or from which he or she rebelled (or is rebelling). And accompanying these kinds of messages are labels like Renaissance, (high and low) baroque, impressionist, cubist, ashcan, minimalist, futurist, constructivist, abstract expressionist, and on and on. It is hard to avoid the conclusion that in this century there are almost as many labels as there are artists. To most viewers, however, these labels are mystifying. More than that, they are intimidating to the point that they inhibit overt expression of response because people regard themselves as incompetent viewers. Just as they have come to regard themselves as incompetent to engage in artistic activity, they have to regard themselves as incompetent viewers. The problem is less acute when they like a work of art because they can then say that they like the colors or the content. It is when they respond negatively and feel they are expected to respond positively that they are puzzled.

To want to appreciate a work of art—in the dictionary sense of *increasing* scope of knowledge and depth of experience—requires going beyond expressions of liking or disliking. If in this literal sense people cannot appreciate art, it is not only because they are ignorant of art history, do not know how to begin to analyze a work of art and their response to it, or are thoroughly intimidated. It is rather that there is nothing in their experience that permits them to identify with the artistic *process*, that process in which one strives to create something "out there" consistent with an expressive of an internal visual conception "in there." Confronted with a work of art, they can only focus on what they see and like or dislike, and they are unable to examine it in terms of why and how the artist produced that particular product. So, for example, they are unaware that what they see is an end product preceded by sketches, experimentation, discarded efforts, and so forth. It is as if what they see came directly from the mind of the artist, as if there was no intervening process.

I am saying something akin to "it takes one to know one." That does not mean that it takes a great artist to appreciate great art, or that only artists, great or otherwise, can appreciate other artists. What it does mean is that if you have any meaningful experience in artistic activity, you are more likely to pursue understanding beyond liking or disliking. If, as is generally the case, you feel absolutely no kinship with what an artist confronts and does, your ability to appreciate his or her products is drastically constrained.

Why is it considered desirable to go beyond expressions of like or dislike of works of art? Why is it considered insufficient, or wrong, or superficial to be satisfied with one's spontaneous affective reactions? On what assumptions do such assertions of "should" and "ought" rest? When we are served a meal that in every way delights our palate and gives rise to exclamations of pleasure, we are not expected to analyze our reactions or to inquire as to the process by which the food was prepared. We know that there was a cook or chef, but we are not about to study the process they employed. And, of course, if we react negatively to the meal, we want to leave the scene, not analyze why that meal turned out so poorly for us. Why should we treat a work of art differently?

The fact is that some people do not do so. If, for example, you are or consider yourself to be a professional or an amateur cook, you will not be content to stay on the level of like or dislike but will seek to understand, to analyze, to fathom how the meal was prepared: its ingredients, the steps in preparation, and so on. You are intrigued, and you seek to understand the sources of your reaction, to enlarge your knowledge. You accord the maker of the meal an artistry, a creativity with which you seek to identify. In this case, eating is not merely a consumatory response but also one that is instrumental in that it leads you to further exploration and intellectual satisfaction of a particular process and product.

Two points here deserve emphasis. The first is that the artistic process manifests itself in myriads of ways and in diverse media. It is not a process that can be kept within the bounds of the conventional arena of "art." As Dewey emphasized, the overlearned tendency to regard artistic activity as something special about special people makes it virtually impossible to recognize its presence in quotidian life. The second point is that appreciating artistic activity and its products depends on, among other things, one's own experience with the particular medium for that particular manifestation of the activity. Experience is not knowledge or facts but activity, engagement, from which knowledge about self, process, and materials gets organized. We are all familiar with the maxim that the more you know the more you need to know. But what that maxim refers to, as in the case of science, is not "knowing" in terms of information, but "knowing" embedded in and derived from active experience. It makes no difference whether you are an astrophysicist reading a report in a professional journal or a chef intrigued by a meal prepared by a stranger. In either case you seek to know more precisely because you have engaged in similar activities. You, so to speak, identify with what the other person has done. If you are not a chef or an astrophysicist, you have no need to know more.

It should occasion no surprise that in regard to artistic activity and its products most people stay on the level of liking or disliking. This is not because they lack what is conventionally called knowledge but because they lack—or feel they lack or have been told they lack—artistic ability. Artistic *activity* is foreign to their experience. Unlike the chef or astrophysicist who have engaged in their respective activities, the ordinary beholder of a work of art has no personal experience that makes knowing about it a necessity. And when I say "ordinary beholder," I mean to include most chefs and astrophysicists. It is hard to exaggerate how effectively we have assimilated the message that artistic activity is a special ability of special people. "Who am *I* to regard *myself* as capable of engaging in artistic activity? Who am *I* to pass judgment on a work of art?" The answer to the first question is that *I* am incapable, and the answer to the second is that *I* am unjustified.

We are here dealing with what Dewey called the "psychological fallacy," or what in this discussion should be called the developmental fallacy: the activities, attitudes, and capabilities that are the outcome of development are considered as having been present in and explaining those outcomes.[3] That is to say, if a person is incapable of engaging in an artistic activity, that incapability is not only an effect but also a cause of that outcome. If that is patently illogical, a nonsequitur, it is unfortunately the most frequent explanation of why only a few people are "artists." Aside from being illogical, it ignores the universality of artistic activity in young children and almost totally underestimates the force of socialization into our culture.

As I was writing this chapter I read one of Russell Baker's incomparable columns in the *New York Times* of December 28, 1988. The column has the heading "Getting Tired of High-Culture Humility":

> I have long intended to become as knowledgeable about the arts as that critic who reviews them for wise-guy weekly publications issued from New York.
>
> Surely you have read his reviews. If he goes to a Rembrandt exhibition, he spends most of the review talking about Rembrandt's debt to Masaccio or Vlaminck or some other painter I have never heard of.
>
> Reviewing the new bodice-ripper by Janette Passionella, he finds the influences of James Fenimore Cooper, Pushkin and Céline giving surprising depth to the book.
>
> Sent to a movie, he awes you with 2,000 words declaring it inferior to the tragedies of Racine, the short stories of Chekhov, the essays of Hilaire Belloc and "The Confessions" of St. Augustine, not to mention the Brahms quartets which he will compare unfavorably with the early works of the Clambake Trio.
>
> This reviewer is familiar with every painting ever painted, every theatrical enterprise ever enterprised, every musical note ever played.
>
> I do not doubt that he is. Experience has proved that some people indeed know everything. As a mere tot, I found them disguised as cruel schoolteachers who wouldn't let me clap the erasers because I couldn't spell "Iroquois" as flawlessly as they could.
>
> When collapsed into middle age, I encountered them as college students on the very best campuses sneering at me for guessing that the "Establishment" was just the figment of some satirist's imagination.

3. This fallacy has been beautifully illustrated and discussed by Patricia Hampl in an essay "The Lax Habits of the Free Imagination" (*New York Times Book Review,* March 5, 1989, p. 1). A piece from one of her books had been chosen to be included in an anthology. When she received her copy of the anthology, she wrote: "I skimmed through my piece. No typos—good. And there, at the end of the selection, in those shivery italic letters reserved for especially significant copy, were the study questions. There were several under the heading 'Questions about Purpose'. One will do: 'Why does Hampl establish her father's significance to her family before she narrates the major incident?' Beats me, I thought. I had no idea what Hampl's purpose was. All the study questions looked quite mad to me.'"

Copious knowledge often produces such meanness of spirit in its possessor. I do not denigrate knowledge because of this, but only wish people who have been assiduous enough to lap it up in vast quantities would be more modest about flaunting the stuff in their mental attics.

I suspect the reviewer cited above is less interested in telling me the cultural news than in reminding me that I don't know Vlaminck from Minsky: that I still haven't got around to reading Pushkin or Céline, that I am physically incapable of reading James Fenimore Cooper without lapsing into coma; that I can distinguish Beethoven's Ninth Symphony only because the Beethoven is noisier, that—

But never mind. You see his game. Like the comedian on "Saturday Night Live" who used to say, "I'm Chevy Chase, and you're not," he is saying, "I am conversant with all art, and you are a pathetically undereducated numbskull."

While his manners may be loutish, the truth of his insinuations cannot be denied. For this reason, I have long meant to marinate myself in music, literature, painting and theatrical expression, until no reviewer could drop the name of an artist or an artwork that was beyond my recognition.

This good work has finally begun, thanks to the recent gift of a compact-disk player which now enables me to hear the finest music performed as purely as though the Philadelphia Orchestra were playing right in my sitting room.

Getting this miracle of Japanese technology to work took six hours and an electrical engineer equipped with a screwdriver scarcely bigger than a needle, but culture should never be cheapened by coming painlessly.

I had a dozen recordings of the music of François Poulenc. Upscale reviewers love to drop the name Poulenc, no matter whose music they are writing about.

I planned to see a movie called "The Naked Gun", and—let me be candid—I thought it would be nice to write a column discussing it at a more sophisticated level than the average daily movie critic can reach. I planned to say something about moments in "The Naked Gun" which were "suffused with the spirit of the ineffable Poulenc."

Naturally, being a journalist of integrity, I wanted to soak up Poulenc's spirit before writing. So Poulenc went on the CD player, and I settled down with James Fenimore Cooper's "Leatherstocking Tales." Yes, killing two birds at once. I thought it would strengthen my proposed movie column to say that "The Naked Gun," while influenced by Poulenc, owed a large debt to Natty Bumppo.

Mine is a small sitting room, measuring 15 by 14 feet. Two is a crowd. Put the Philadelphia Orchestra in there and even the deadly James Fenimore Cooper cannot overpower the racket and induce his famous coma. Cooper and Poulenc combined, however, can produce a headache as pure as a Giotto circle and as thunderous as Milton's mighty line.

Needing instant relief, I squelched Poulenc, dropped Cooper and ran to see "The Naked Gun." It can't hold a candle to "The Castle of Otranto."

Mr. Baker is an artist. He knows well what is involved in giving form to an internal idea or vision. He understands and respects the nature and struggles of artistic activity. He is no philistine. But in that brief column he has articulated not only why people are so intimidated in their responses to the products or artistic activity, but also why the possibility of engaging in artistic activity is so alien to their self-appraisal. You could say that the theme of the column is that if people are made to feel ignorant and incapable, they end up ignorant and incapable. He makes his point with humor and satire, expressing in a literary form what most people have experienced. It deserves emphasis that Mr. Baker is not disparaging artistic activity. Quite the contrary, he is indicating the way in which we are taught to pass judgment on that activity, whether it is our activity or that of others.

It is part of my argument that Mr. Baker could not have said what he did if he himself were not an artist—if he did not experience and understand what artistic activity entails or requires. Possessed of such understanding, he can see how the cultural messages he so skillfully undercuts say nothing at all about artists and artistic activity.

Why is it so difficult to accept the assertion—or at least to discuss it as a serious possibility—that artistic activity is a normal, universal feature of human beings? Why do we regard it as a special activity of special people? Why is the prepotent tendency to judge the products of the activity according to culturally determined criteria of worthiness (for example, saying that Russell Baker is no Mark Twain, or that Grandma Moses is no Cézanne) an obstacle to recognizing its presence in "ordinary" people? When and why do we change our minds about what people are capable of? Is it not obvious in human history that conceptions of human abilities have altered as worldviews derived from cultural change have changed? If that is obvious, should it be no less obvious that our current conceptions will be changed in the future? I shall have more to say about these matters later, but here I want briefly to note a current instance of a change in how conceptions of the abilities of a certain group of people are undergoing change. If this instance is not about artistic activity, it nevertheless contains the germ of a rather complete answer to the questions above. So let me talk about black quarterbacks in college and professional football.

As recently as five years ago there were virtually no black quarter-

backs in professional football. (I do not pretend to encyclopedic knowledge of the rosters of the professional teams. There may have been one
or two, but they were not "first team" players.) There were many superb
black running backs, linebackers, and linemen. Indeed, the percentage
of starting blacks was far greater than what the number of blacks in the
general population would have suggested.

Today whites are a "minority" in professional football. Why were
there no black quarterbacks? The answer, rarely publicly discussed, was
that blacks lacked the cognitive skills necessary to perform as quarterback—a position that more than any other requires the individual to be
aware of a multitude of factors and possibilities, to think and act quickly
and skillfully, and by his display of competence to inspire confidence in
his teammates. For example, he must be able in a matter of seconds to
read or "diagnose" the other team's defenses and, if need be, again
almost instantly, change the play to be used. To my knowledge, no one
has seen fit to study and analyze the phenomenology of a quarterback's
thinking or problem solving, but no one who has played football or has
been a coach underestimates the complex factors a quarterback has to
take into account. Dealing with that complexity was considered beyond
the blacks who aspired to that position. That conclusion, of course,
never sat well with blacks, although I do not doubt that many of them
agreed with the conventional wisdom if only because it was but one of
many such messages that had been subtly or blatantly conveyed to them
in their lives. So, for all practical purposes, there were no black quarterbacks in college and professional football until about five years ago.
That situation has dramatically altered.

I have not used the example of black quarterbacks to illustrate or
indict racism; the evil consequences of racism need no elaboration or
confirmation from me. I brought it up for two reasons. The first is that
it is a clear example of how our conception of people's abilities is embedded in, suffused, and reinforced by culture. If we know that is the case
in racism, we should also know or at least suspect that it is true where
racism is not at issue. Racism is an *obvious* example, but does it not
require that we ask about the *nonobvious* ways culture may be misreading the potential of people? I could have used sex discrimination as an
example—again, not for the purpose of indicting it but rather to suggest that culture, any culture, rests on axioms about the nature of
people's capacities.

From my perspective, racism and sex discrimination are double-
edged swords. On the one hand, they identify the central issues; on the

other hand, they are so specific as to prevent us from seeing these issues in a more general way, a way that would alter how we think about people's abilities regardless of what group they belong to. That is the significance of where one stands in regard to artistic activity as a universal feature of human beings. The culture says that only special people have what it takes to engage in this special activity. I, obviously, have been arguing otherwise.

This brings me to the second reason I employed the black quarterback (or gender discrimination) example. Both are examples of what I have elsewhere (Sarason, 1977) described as a distinctive feature of the post–World War II era: diverse groups' redefinition of themselves as resources—blacks, women, old people, the physically handicapped, nurses, students, and so on. What they all have in common is the stance: "No longer will we view ourselves as the society has heretofore viewed us. We are capable of much more than what the conventional wisdom has held." Each group served as its own advocate, and sought and obtained the support of other constituencies. They were articulate, and frequently militant representatives for their cause, which was nothing less than a claim that they were capable of doing and being more than what they had done or been.

To a discernible extent, they have changed attitudes and expectations in people generally. In regard to artistic activity as a feature of human capabilities, there are no organized advocates or constituencies who clearly seek to redefine how we regard what people are capable of but have no opportunity to demonstrate; that is, that they are rendered incapable of engaging in and deriving satisfaction from a uniquely human characteristic. Someone once said that mandatory retirement was a form of legally sanctioned human abuse because it prevented people from doing what they were capable of doing. That statement was made before mandatory retirement was legislated out of existence by federal law. That came about less because of a sea-swell change in societal attitudes than because of the size and force of advocacy groups in the political arena.

I regard rendering people incapable of engaging in and appreciating artistic activity as a form of human abuse. And I use the word *abuse* in the dictionary sense: "to use so as to injure or damage." It is, of course, not a conscious form of abuse because if it were, there would be groups opposed to it. And it is not a form of abuse whose consequences are visible or palpable or violate cultural norms. And that is the point: ours is a culture that, while it accords respect to artistic activity and "artists," denies that this activity is one that all people are capable of. It respects creativity, but it asserts that all but a few people are creative. It purports to understand, and it even envies, the satisfactions that come from artistic activity, from the experience of putting one's personal stamp, one's internal vision, on some configurated, externalized object or space. But those satisfactions are those of special people with special ability. Our society is a prisoner of the view that artists are those who call themselves artists or whose products have received the imprimatur of museums, galleries, or art critics. It recognizes "folk art" and "primitive art," but in so labeling them it exposes the value judgment that they are of lesser quality, worth, or cultural significance. "Great art" is the seal of worth. And by these labels the import of the activity and its products for our conceptions of human capability goes unexamined. Worse yet, the role of creativity in human existence, the consequences for people of feeling uncreative, the ways in which the cards are stacked to make people feel they are uncreative, go unexamined.

Nothing in what I have said should be interpreted as suggesting that everyone is capable of becoming a recognized artist by conventional standards. What I have been saying can be put in several sentences:

1. All people are capable of engaging in artistic activity.
2. Artistic activity, regardless of choice of medium, is an unrivaled way of deriving satisfaction by giving external form to an internal conception or vision unique to the individual.
3. The satisfactions from the activity, the energizing and propelling consequences of the activity, are, can, and should be independent of the level and complexity of the process and its products. The activity is self-reinforcing.
4. Our culture very effectively extinguishes in most people a desire to engage in artistic activity, not only "damaging or injuring" their view of themselves and their activity but also rendering them incapable of appreciating the activity and its products in others.
5. Where one stands in regard to artistic activity says a great deal about one's conception of the nature of human nature in its transactions with culture. Precisely because of the inevitability and force of those transactions, culture is omnipresent in and around the human organism.

My experiences force me to conclude that many, if not most, readers may feel that I am making a mountain out of a molehill. Few things contribute more to such a reaction than the mammothly overlearned tendency to associate art and artists with imagery of museums, galleries, and "great art." This tendency is in all respects identical in consequences to that of associating education with imagery of buildings and classrooms, as if those were the only places where education took place. The effort on the part of some thinkers and observers to distinguish between schooling and education has had little or no impact on people generally and on those responsible for educational policy and change in particular. As a result, we rivet on what goes on inside of school buildings and ignore the world outside.

As I discuss in *Schooling in America,* as long as we maintain our narrow conception of where education takes place, the quality of education will remain as poor as it is, a hypothesis that explains past and present inadequacies and predicts future ones. Similarly, as long as our thinking continues to be determined by grossly narrow imagery of art and artists, we will fail to comprehend how people are denied (unwittingly, of course) the satisfactions of engaging in artistic activity, regardless of level of accomplishment or chosen medium. Just as conventional schooling denies most students the satisfactions derived from productive learning, the conventional view of artistic activity denies people the experience of growth in externalizing or objectifying in a configurated way an internal conception. It is a denial of the experience of creativity, a denial that impoverishes self-regard and understanding of our world. It is a denial that people accept, at the same time that what is denied shows up in the only arena available: fantasy.

There is another obstacle to serious discussion of artistic activity as an important characteristic and need of people. It is present when a person concludes, as I did, that the universal axiom that education best takes place in encapsulated classrooms in encapsulated schools is largely, if not wholly, invalid. When you arrive at that point, you see that dramatic changes in how and where schooling occurs will have to be made. That perception can be overwhelming. Changing your worldview is always upsetting. It is no different when you pursue the consequences of taking seriously that artistic activity is part of our birthright. You now see the world differently and you now see how that world should change. Artistic activity is a process in which by transforming materials in accord with an internal conception the individual and the materials undergo transformation. We are used to hearing that people climb Mt. Everest because "it is there." Someone else said that the artist makes whatever he or she makes because "it is *not* there." It is "inside" and he or she seeks to put it "out there" in order to fulfill or satisfy a uniquely personal need.

9 ◆ WRITING

I n previous chapters I have emphasized how difficult it is to regard
artistic activity as a universal feature of human beings. That difficulty has diverse sources, among which three are especially effective. The first is our prepotent tendency to associate artistic activity with
individuals who call themselves artists, or whom we, through absorp-
tion of our culture, call artists. This is like saying that teaching is an
activity that *only* classroom teachers employ. The second source is the
failure to distinguish between artistic activity and our aesthetic or affective response to the products of the activity. If we do not like or approve
of such a product, we are not likely to seek to understand or analyze the
activity. Or, what is far more frequent, if such a product elicits no
response, we "pay it no mind," and the activity goes unnoticed. We are
not schooled to seek to identify the presence of the activity independent
of our aesthetic-affective reaction to its products. It took a Freud to alert
us to the diverse ways in which sexual activity manifests itself in the play
and behavior of young children, forcing us to look at children and
sexual activity far more closely than had previously been the case. If
today we are more sensitive than ever before to the manifestations of
sexual activity, that kind of sensitivity to artistic activity is generally
absent. The third source of our difficulty in regarding the universality
of artistic activity is the most potent of all: the many ways in which the
culture instills in people the belief that they are not capable of engaging
in and deriving satisfaction from artistic activity, regardless of the level
of performance, that is, the complexity and quality of the activity. Far
from being nurtured, the *development* of artistic activity is ignored or
blunted.

In this chapter I shall pursue this third source in a personal way. I
shall draw upon my experience as a writer and as someone who has
spent almost a half-century helping undergraduate and graduate student use language as a way of giving ordered expression to their
thoughts. I am a teacher of psychology, not of writing, but the fact is, as
the reader well knows, instructors require papers (long and short),

graduate students have to write dissertations (among other things), and instructors then have to read and evaluate them. No student of mine has ever regarded a writing assignment from me as an exercise in artistic activity. It simply does not occur to my students that I am asking them to engage in an activity that is quintessentially artistic: selecting, utilizing, organizing materials from a particular medium (language) that is isomorphic, with internal thoughts, imagery, and feelings. Indeed, there is an unverbalized contract between student and instructor: plagiarizing is off limits. No copying. Your task as student is to think about and use the materials of language in ways that externalize what internally *you* want to say. The paper is you, yourself, a personal imprimatur. It is your creation. In regard to language you are in the same position as a sculptor faced with a block of marble. The media are different but the goals are similar: to chip or hammer away at a medium to make something that squares with what is in your mind's eye—to transform what is "in there."

It was from this perspective that last year I gave the following assignment to students in an undergraduate seminar: "For next week I want you to make and come in with a painting, two-feet square, of a disturbed family: mother, father, a son, and a daughter." The words *disturbed family* had meaning to them and were relevant to previous discussions in the seminar. Their reactions were predictable: consternation, disbelief, exclamations that they were not artists, and by what criteria would I grade their efforts? After listening to their reactions, I made several points. Why do we automatically associate the artistic process with visual art? If I had asked them to write a paper on some feature of disturbed families, was I not asking them to engage in an artistic activity? Could they, could anyone, write such a paper without seeking clarity about what they wanted to say—toying with ideas, imagery, concepts and configuring them in some way—and then wrestling with the medium of language to get it to express what they wanted to say? Was writing such a paper devoid of the need or requirement to be creative? No, they did not have to come in next week with a painting, but in writing the paper I would assign I hoped they would reflect on what they meant when they said or felt they were not artists. I shall have more to say later about these matters in regard to students. I turn now to my own experience and development in writing.

I have no memory whatsoever of anyone in my precollege years going over with me anything I had written. In fact, I cannot recall ever writing, or being asked to write, anything that could by the broadest definition be considered creative. Although I have to assume that my memory is far from perfect, I have to conclude that writing as a form of personal expression was for all practical purposes absent from the curriculum. For two decades in the post–World War II era, I spent a lot of time in a lot of elementary and middle schools, and I never observed a single instance where the process and activity of writing—using and organizing language to express internal thoughts and feelings—was discussed. When I hear today that most high school graduates cannot write a clear letter, regardless of its purpose, I am puzzled (really angry) by the explicit criticisms of both teachers and students.

For one thing, the obvious fact is that teachers are not expected to spend time in a crowded curriculum helping students begin to understand *and* experience what is involved in the process of writing. In addition, little or nothing in the preparation of teachers gives them an understanding of writing as a developmental process that needs nurturing or stimulation in a one-on-one relationship. Writing as an art is foreign to their thinking and practice in regard to their students. Learning to write becomes a technical skill requiring students to use and organize language to meet criteria valued by others. Students are not asked to write about what interests them or what they may really want to say, presumably because it is thought that students lack the technical skills and that therefore writing as an artistic activity is impossible for them. It cannot be recognized that the emphasis on the technical-motor aspect may extinguish or prevent students' interest in writing. I have yet to meet a teacher, or a teacher of teachers, who has read Koch's work with children as poets. I am sure there are some who have read his work. In general, however, the idea of students as literary artists is foreign to the educational arena. Let us not forget that the literary artistry of Koch's elementary school children in Harlem was due to an "outsider," not someone indigenous to the school. And let us not forget that what this outsider demonstrated was that literary artistry required development, a nurtured unfolding of complex mental activity that put a unique stamp on the products. Technique was not unimportant but it was in the service of a creative effort.

If I learned anything about writing in my public school days, it was that I wanted to have as little to do with it as possible. There were those exercises in *penmanship,* making interlocking circles which could not, must not, go above or below two parallel lines. Page after page of this, leading me and my teachers to conclude that I was a hopeless case, incapable of fine motoric movements. And then were those endless exercises of copying letters on sentences from the blackboard, and again I demonstrated my inability to write clearly. And here was the point: I had to learn to copy faithfully, literally to reproduce what someone else did, and be judged by the standards of others. Did I have something to say I wanted to write about? Why on earth should I have felt I had anything to say and write? It should occasion no surprise that my experience of inadequacy in using pen or pencil for the purposes of writing "clearly" made the occasional assignments to make a picture or drawing an exercise in negative self-regard. If I can write about these experiences today with amusement, it is another example of human masking or selectively distorting a long-standing anxiety or conflict.

There was no "literary" tradition in my immigrant family, nuclear or extended. There was respect for learning, but that meant going to school, learning what you were told to learn, getting good grades, ultimately "making something of yourself." Nobody read stories to me, but early on I became a reader and a library-goer. Westerns, sports stories, Tom Swift, and the Street and Smith pulp magazines were my average fare. The books by Fenimore Cooper were the only ones I read that were above average in quality. Reading at home gave me a world the polar opposite of that contained in my school books. The two worlds never intersected.

Words and language came to fascinate me largely because for two years in junior high I had a teacher who taught Latin as a way of understanding English. That our language had "foreign" origins, that if I knew Latin I might be able to guess the meaning of English words I had not encountered before, and that looking up words in the dictionary could be interesting, intrigued me no end. I understand why Latin came to be regarded as a dead language, taught as it usually was as a memory game, unrelated to anything in a child's experience. But for me, Latin was alive. I am in no way suggesting that my experience with Latin had anything to do with my later interest in writing. What it *did* do was to make words and language interesting to me. They had an attraction for me. They were not "only" words and language.

My mother decided I should learn to play the piano. This, I can assure the reader, was not based on any perception that I was interested in doing so or had a special talent. The fact is that I willingly went along with the decision because I liked to listen to music and to sing. If I went along willingly, even somewhat eagerly, it was only because I wanted to learn to play the popular music of the day. I quickly learned to read music. And I only mildly resented the seemingly endless finger exercises. I think it fair to say that I understood the necessity of those exercises. What I did not understand after a year was why I was given simple pieces, the equivalent of "Oh Oh, Puff Puff" in reading primers, to practice and play. I wanted to play Irving Berlin, George Gershwin, and others whose songs I heard on the radio. "Why can't I learn to play what I want to play?" I would ask my mother. Her reply was quite predictable: what I wanted to play was not "good" music. I never took this up with Mr. Saslow, my teacher. You did what teachers told you to do, period. They, like parents, know best. Besides, Mr. Saslow was a constricted, unsmiling, uninspiring person. When I look back at those several years under his tutelage, I cannot remember a time when he tried to get to know me, talk with me, get me thinking about feeling, expression, nuances, and touch. There was so much that I wanted to express through music, but it was forbidden fruit.

On the day I am writing these words I received a letter from a friend, Bruce Thomas. The first sentence quoted below from this letter is in reference to something I discussed in *The Making of an American Psychologist:*

> I was intrigued with your discussion of the use of the "I" in writing. A month or so ago, I was in battle in Minnesota on the issue of this report I wrote on the state of Minnesota's children; one of the points of contention was style, and in particular its informality as carried by the use of "we" instead of the impersonal and putatively authoritative third person. One of the people in the meeting said, "It's not professional, the way you're writing." And I was mute; I felt like Billy Budd, so choked with rage that words got immobilized and all I wanted to do was strike out in rage. All, finally, I could say was, "This report was written by human beings for human beings. The language ought to reflect that."

If the musical pieces I had to play were really written by composers for the likes of me, Mr. Saslow carefully kept that a secret. I have no doubt that Mr. Saslow regarded me as a bright young boy who had no musical talent and could never play the way he played. And I have no doubt that he perceived correctly that I did not particularly enjoy playing the piano. What he did not perceive was that I loved music, and that it should have been his goal to help me use the piano to give expression to the feelings and fantasies inside of me. That the music he had me play was written by people to give overt form to what was inside of them was a thought he never once articulated. The composers and I had nothing in common.

The fantasy, and that is what it was, of becoming a writer had nothing to do with previous interests and past performance. It had a lot to do with the fact that at age fourteen I contracted polio in both arms; the right arm became a dead weight, and the left arm developed a marked weakness in the shoulder joint. Both arms were raised, benediction-style, by a brace that enveloped me from the waist up. The relevant point here is that I was left with fantasy as my major source of expression and enjoyment. What would I do? What would I become? What did I *want* to become? The answer to the last question was clear: I wanted to become famous. There was obviously no longer any point to fantasizing about becoming a famous athlete, ordinarily number one on my priority list. (I do not think there was a number two or three.) How and why I hit upon becoming a playwright I truly do not know, but I developed an interest in the New York theatrical scene. I read plays and any column or news item that had to do with Broadway: actors, directors, producers, gossip columnists (such as Walter Winchell and Leonard Lyons). My fantasies were utterly devoid of any idea of what my plays would be about. They were fantasies about celebrity and fortune. To make it on the Broadway scene would be possible only through writing. From a purely physical standpoint, writing was the only medium available to me. But I wrote nothing. The playwright fantasies diminished only somewhat. Two years after I contracted polio I entered a local college.

I had to write papers for various courses. Here too, as in high school, no one ever sat down and discussed with me what was involved, what one's obligations to readers were, in writing clearly. What they did do was tell me whether what I wrote was "right or wrong," of if there were omissions of substance, or whether certain points were unclear or needed elaboration. In short, they focused on the degree to which I was factual. No one ever encouraged or discouraged me to write. From my discussions with other students I found out two things about myself. First, unlike most of them, writing held no terror for me. Second, I liked the writing assignments. There was something about picking up the pencil and *thinking* that was enjoyable. How should I begin? What did I want to say? Was this the right adjective to use? Was I saying what I wanted to say in what, for me at least, seemed a "literary" fashion? The fact is that I became a kind of writing consultant to other students for whom going from internal thought to written language was excruciatingly painful. This was another example of "in the land of the blind, the one-eyed astigmatic man is king."

Writing as a kind of recreational form of activity (that is, unrelated to course requirements) came about by the confluence of two factors. The first was my immersion in radical politics. I joined the Young People's Socialist League, then the Socialist Workers' Party, and then the Workers' Party. Leon Trotsky had become one of my heroes. The second factor was the student newspaper. Our task was to make sure that the Trotskyite view of the world was represented in the newspaper. More correctly, we had to counteract the influence of the Communist party on the pages of that newspaper. I got on the staff of the paper, and that meant writing on diverse topics. I should disabuse the reader of any idea that I saw myself as a writer. Rather, I saw myself for what I was: a propagandist. However, I was aware that I enjoyed the process of thinking and writing. No one had to tell me that sculpting language to represent thoughts and imagery was both trying and satisfying. The possibility that I was engaged in an artistic activity, albeit on a "primitive" level, could never enter my mind, and the same was the case for anyone who read my stuff.

The time I spent writing increased dramatically when I was elected editor of the paper. There were times when it felt as if I was writing the entire paper, which was no burden at all. But there was one thing I did that convinced me that writing was something special in my life. I attended the weekly meetings of the student government and wrote up the discussions and decisions in news articles. Because they were news articles they could not contain my personal views and observations of the participants. Put in another way, the news was factual but it was not *my* truth. So what I did weekly was to write an anonymous column describing the meetings. I wrote the columns as if I were a man from Mars watching the proceedings, which were as hilarious as they were serious. And it was the hilarious that I wrote about, making sure that I no less than others was the butt of humor. The response to the columns was beyond my expectations. The important thing, however, was the realization that writing was the only way I could express what I thought and felt. That, I can assure the reader, did not mean that I entertained thoughts of a writing career. I was intent on going to graduate school to become a psychologist. Yes, someday I would write plays and become famous, but first things first.

Insofar as graduate school was concerned, writing was an advanced version of college. Whatever I wrote was to satisfy my instructors. I was socialized to view writing as an activity that required impersonality, objectivity, and affective neutrality. And of the hundreds, perhaps thousands, of journal articles and books I had to read, you could count on the fingers of your two hands instances of the use of "I." This did not trouble me. I did not feel put upon or frustrated. I dutifully and willingly wrote the way I was told to write. This explains, but only in part, why I found William James and Sigmund Freud so interesting to read. I tried (unsuccessfully) to read everything they had written, far beyond the paltry number of pages required by my instructors. They, I recognized, were writers unafraid to say what they thought and felt. When I would read them, I found myself conjuring up pictures of what they were like as individuals. Such conjuring never intruded into my thoughts when I read articles in scientific journals. Those articles were immensely valuable in my development as a psychologist. But in some inchoate way I knew that scientific writing was not the kind that would be expressive of *me*. I wanted to become a scientific psychologist, do research, write it up for the journals, and thereby gain recognition to satisfy my ambitiousness. The truth is that that scenario was powered more by ambition than by my equally strong need to use written language as a form of personal expression.

In my first position after receiving the doctorate in 1942, I did scientific research, and I started to write a play. That the play deserved oblivion goes without saying. I put my all into it, was exhilarated by the process, but after reading it several times I had to conclude that it was quite amateurish. Of course it was, but I know now that I was judging the play by the most unrealistic criteria. I never asked myself why I should expect that my second serious effort (my first one was in college) should be other than amateurish. I knew that artistic activity is a developmental process that should take place in a context both instructive and encouraging, a context in which one learns the tools of the trade through and with others. Ensconced as I was as a psychologist in a state institution in rural Connecticut during World War II, there was no one, no context, to keep the tiny literary flame alive in me.

The most important point is that I did not have the courage to show the play to anyone for fear of ridicule. Who was I to regard myself as a budding playwright? Would I not be regarded as unrealistic and grandiose? Would not my imaginary critics conclude that I lacked artistic talent? I and my imaginary critics were using criteria of quality and achievement guaranteed to stifle, indeed abort, further development, criteria I know now that extinguishes the desire to engage in artistic activity. We are used to hearing that "if it is really in you, your artistry will become manifest." That is what I call the platonic view of artistic activity: some people have that artistic essence which develops and manifests itself regardless of soil; most people lack that essence so that regardless of soil it will never show itself. And "show itself" means meeting culturally determined and elevated criteria of quality. It does not mean that an individual has created something that, however short it falls of these cultural criteria, nevertheless reflects a serious effort to use a medium to express internal imagery in an ordered way. If the mountain climber fails to scale Mt. Everest, he feels disappointed, but he does not regret the effort. I never wrote another play.

I did, however, publish my research studies. The fun in research is not in collecting data but in formulating an issue or question and then writing up your results. (You can pay assistants to collect the data, but you cannot pay them to think or write for you.) The fun inheres in figuring out the different meanings in the data, how they do or do not fit in with your initial formulations, and how you can put into words what you think these meanings are. I say fun but it is also an encompassing struggle. On the one hand, you know what you hoped the data would reveal and, on the other hand, it is usually the case that the data do not uniformly confirm those hopes. How do you put it all together? How do you configure the results so that they make sense to you? How do you now use language to make your sense clear to the reader?

I am not aware of any attempt to obtain the phenomenology of the researcher who is writing up his or her research. When we read the published product, we are not interested in phenomenology. We want to know the questions being asked, the methodology employed, and how the data confirm, disconfirm, or muddy the issues involved. Does it all make sense—by which we mean, does it hang together logically or are there gaps, omissions, errors, misinterpretations? If the stance we adopt when we read the article is understandable, indeed necessary, it is nevertheless a stance that effectively obscures the artistic activity inherent in writing up the study. The researcher, no less than conventionally regarded artists, struggles not only to obtain an internal, configured picture of meanings, to *figure* out what should go with what, what to select or exclude, but also how to use language to convey that configured picture. I daresay that no researcher who begins to write up his or her study escapes the realization that bending language to one's purposes is no simple affair, certainly not one explicable by the rules of ordinary logic. There are, I have concluded, two kinds of researchers: one dreads the writing up process, and the other luxuriates in the interplay between internal pictures and their objectification through language. In one case writing is as pleasurable as pulling teeth; in the other it is as challenging as fashioning teeth.

Researchers do not view themselves as literary artists. Hemingway, Faulkner, Updike, and others—*they* are writers. I have quizzed researchers on this point and three points inevitably arise. First, when they think of literary artists, what comes to their minds are recognized writers. Second, writing up research is a creative endeavor that probably is not unlike that experienced by these recognized writers, although the researchers never thought of these underlying similarities of process. Third, the researchers would feel very uncomfortable saying they were at some level literary artists, as if to say so were a form of imperialistic arrogance. One of these researchers, a renowned individual, said: "You are absolutely right. Anyone who concludes from reading one of my papers that he understands what I did and experienced in writing that paper is dead wrong. Someone once said that the hallmark of a pro is that he or she makes it look easy. I am told that my papers are relatively easy to read. That says less about my reasoning powers, my scientific credentials, and more about my unbounded respect for my ideas which, because of that respect, I want to make sure are not subverted by language. What the reader reads is an end product that simply does not reflect the complexity and creativity of the process from which it emerged." I have no doubt that if we compared the phenomenology of researchers as writers with that of artists in any medium, the similarities would be obvious. Research articles differ widely on many dimensions: organization, handling of transitions, theme development, use of imagery and analogy, sentence structure, repetition for emphasis—what we subsume under the hard-to-define label "style." The correlation between style and scientific quality and impact is far from perfect.

On countless occasions I have heard researchers say, "I am no artist." Any they mean what they say. This is another example of how a culturally determined and reinforced narrow conception of artistic activity leads people to misperceive and misevaluate themselves and others. Where there should be a perception of kinship there is a perception of an unbridgeable difference. Winston Churchill once quipped that England and America were two countries divided by a common language. In regard to artistic activity we use a common language to divide what in nature is not divisible: art and artistic activity are one thing, everything else is something else. Differences in phenotype are assumed to reflect differences in genotype, an unreflective assumption as mischievous in practical consequences as it is unwarranted in logic.

So I wrote research papers. It did not take me long to realize that one factor diminished the satisfaction I derived from writing journal articles. This factor in part explains why researchers have difficulty seeing themselves as engaging in literary artistry. I refer to the fact that there is almost always a prescribed format for journal articles. There are limitations on length and an unverbalized but very effective "rule" that you write impersonally. Using "I" is verboten. You write as if what you have written is independent of and irrelevant to your feelings and judgments about the significance of what you did. It would perhaps be more correct to say that you are permitted to include only those aspects of your thinking most relevant to your hypotheses and data. No researcher would deny that the written report contains a small sample of all that he or she thought about what the data may mean. Put in another way, if the researcher was not confined to a prescribed format, the written report would read differently, very differently. The prescribed format is not without its justifications, but my point is that it restricts and stifles literary artistry. This is not to say that the scientific value of the articles would be enhanced if there were no prescribed format, although that possibility cannot be blithely dismissed. It is to say that the personal satisfaction the researcher would derive from writing would be far greater than it is. The worth of an effort does not reside only in the reactions of others to it.

After I left my position as psychologist in an institution for mentally retarded individuals, I wanted to bring together all that I had experienced and thought I had learned. I had something I wanted to say that I thought the world should hear. Obviously, I could not do this in the usual formal article or series of articles. Yet who was I to write a *book*? It was an intimidating thought. No less than most people, the phrase "writing a book" conjured up imagery of arrogance, skill, and creativity that daunted me for a couple of years. The mammoth obstacle was that I wanted to write in a personal way, the only way that would allow me to say what I experienced—the conclusions I had reached even though I could not buttress them with "hard data." How could I write without the personal pronoun *I* appearing rather frequently on the pages? I succumbed to the convention of avoiding *I* and wrote the book in an impersonal style. It was quite a struggle because I was constantly aware of how much of me was missing, how hiding behind the impersonal pronoun restricted expressing *my* truths.

Writing is never easy. Getting language to be even semi-isomorphic with internal thoughts and imagery may not be as bad as Chinese torture, but it is on the same side of the continuum of pain. That is why, I assume, someone once said that artists obviously have a monopoly on masochism which, let us not forget, is the seeking of pleasure through pain. For me, writing that book was difficult because I was using a style I felt was inappropriate to my needs. I did not have a Koch or a Schaefer-Simmern to encourage me to write it my way, to satisfy my internal vision and conception. The fact is that the book was quite influential in the field. Although that was no end gratifying—I was not about to look a gift horse in the mouth—I was far from satisfied with the way the book was written. Too much of me was missing.

It was not until mid-career, after writing many journal articles and about a dozen books in the conventional way, that I got up the courage to say "no more." I began to write in the first person. Writing became a joy, a passion, the one activity that made me feel that I was using all of me creatively. When people asked me what I did, I said I was a psychologist. I considered myself a writer but I was ashamed to say that because I expected (I think correctly) that it would be viewed as arrogance to regard myself as a literary artist in the same general category as Freud, Hemingway, O'Connor, and Faulkner. I was not about to have to explain that I do not have delusions of grandeur. (I do have the most grandiose fantasies, but they are under control.) I was not in the same league as those writers, but I engaged in the same artistic-creative process and, I assume, derived similar satisfactions from it.

Let me now turn to graduate students. Two features of their approach to writing are noteworthy. The first is the almost complete absence of anticipatory pleasure. The second is their insecurity about what to include where. They know the prescribed structure the paper or dissertation should have, but they are largely at sea in deciding how to begin each section, what to emphasize, how to emphasize, and how to bring it all together. Some of these students have done a fair amount of fiction writing, but even for them writing the dissertation is an exercise in dread. Only one of them insisted, successfully, that he be permitted to write in the way he felt comfortable. He was the exception, whose insistence explains most of the difficulties of all the others—that powerful, overlearned attitude that one has to conform to (the equivalent in the visual arts to copying reality) the requirements of others, that one has to leave oneself out of the picture. What is striking and fascinating is the wide gulf between this attitude and how in conversation with me students *talk* about the study they have done. When they talk the "I" appears, they become fluent, and what they really feel about the study becomes clear. It is when they take pencil to paper (or today use the word processor) that the personal disappears and the search for "right" ways of conforming to convention takes over. When literary critics say pejoratively that someone's writing has all of the dryness and impersonality of "academic writing," and to read that writing is a sure cure for insomnia, they are indicating a socialization process more than the artistic deficits of the writer. This socialization process is by no means peculiar to writing.

My last book was my autobiography. I did not write it because I thought my life was distinctive or that my contributions were so outstanding. No one asked me to write it. The main reason I wrote it was to counter the ahistorical view that most psychologists have of their field. I used my personal and professional experience to illuminate the diverse factors contributing to psychology as it is today. I have never derived so much pleasure and satisfaction from writing. In the tradition of converts, I suggested to some senior, outstanding scholars in different areas of psychology that they write their autobiographies. It was not an idle suggestion, because I knew that each of these eminent psychologists was dissatisfied with the directions psychology had taken in the post–World War II era and that each had given a lot of thought to these transformations. And they were people who had written scores of articles and books. In almost every instance their response to my suggestion was in two parts. The first was, yes, they had given much thought to writing their professional autobiographies. The second was, no, they felt unable to write in the personal way an autobiography required. As one of them said: "God knows how many words I have written in my lifetime but I can't remember ever using the pronoun *I*. It would take too much out of me to try, and I really feel that the end product would be lousy, by my standards and by those of others. No thank you." These were highly successful people for whom scientific writing held no terror. And yet they all denied that they had something to say, something they wanted to say, something no less important than anything else they had written. But saying it required a personal stance, a kind of artistry, an ordered expressiveness with which they felt unable to cope. One could ask: so what? Given the fact that mediocre writing is not in short supply, why add more of that quality to overcrowded library shelves? Because something can be done, is that sufficient reason to do it?

These questions are beside the point, which is that when individuals of their caliber, personal and intellectual, are unable or unwilling to withstand the pressure to write in conformity with a prescriptive convention (that is, scientific writings), we begin to understand why from early on in the life of most people, literary artistry is stifled or extinguished. It is fair to say that children are not taught to write because anyone thinks that they are capable of using written language creatively, however "primitive" the product. Writing is taught as a technical skill, not as an activity giving expression to what is personal. To be convinced on this point one needs to sit in classrooms and observe what children are learning about the functions of writing, what writing is intended to accomplish. You will see little or nothing, mostly nothing, that contradicts the assertion that writing is not intended to be a form of truly personal expression. If you made those observations and then read Kenneth Koch's book on writing poetry in a ghetto elementary school, the difference between writing as a creative and writing as a narrow utilitarian activity would be obvious. Why anyone should expect children to want to write, to like to write, is beyond my comprehension. Everything in their experience conspires to make writing a chore to be undertaken only at the point of a gun.

10 ◆ THE PREDICTABLE
FAILURE OF
EDUCATIONAL REFORM

I assume that the reader, having come this far in the book, has been willing seriously to examine, if not to accept, the proposition that artistic activity is a universal human attribute. What questions or problems then arise? Let us not gloss over the fact that any time a change in worldview about the nature of human nature begins to occur, a host of perplexities arises, not the least of which revolve around intended and unintended consequences. It is one thing to attain clarity of values and purposes; it is quite another to adopt a course of action consistent with those values and purposes. I am not referring here to the turmoil in accustomed social arrangements that changes in worldview stir up. That kind of turmoil is completely predictable, in outline at least.

The history of science is not understandable apart from several bedrock assumptions: the more you know the more you need to know; things are never as simple as they appear; and the human capacity to be deceived and seduced by passion and partisanship is bottomless. So, in regard to the argument developed in previous chapters I cannot avoid the question: if the major theme of this book were to be taken seriously, what conceptual and pedagogical problems would have to be faced and clarified if we are to avoid being victims of "the more things change, the more they remain the same"? How consistent our actions are to our intended purposes is no less important in some ultimate sense than accepting the proposition that artistic activity is a universal human attribute. As we shall see, in regard to action our knowledge is inadequate and the problems immense. At the very least we must attempt to identify the problems. Some of them have already been posed by others, although mostly they have gone relatively unnoticed or have not been taken seriously.

Let us start with science education, which may seem a strange place to begin a discussion of artistic activity. I start there for several reasons. The first is the undeniable fact that science as activity and accomplishment has come to pervade our worldview as never before. In the population generally, indeed in all nations on this earth, science has come to be regarded (by some with enthusiasm and by some with reluctance) as a way of comprehending man and the world. It is not only a matter of according respect to science but of recognizing that daily living has been and will be altered by science. If many people do not understand how this came about, if they are mystified by what they perceive as the arcane ways of scientific thinking and research, if they see scientists as special kinds of people, they also accept science as a desirable influence in their lives. It is axiomatic that science is good. If all this is old hat to the reader, it needs to be said that it was not so long ago that this axiom was *not* axiomatic.

The second reason I start with science education is a more recent development: the belief that it is not enough to respect science or to passively accept its accomplishments but that people generally have to *understand* science to some degree. Just as for millennia cultures had as their major educational task instilling in the young a particular theology and cosmogony—their way of understanding and dealing with their world—so the intellectual community has sought to insure that young people are exposed to the ways of science. With the legitimation of universal compulsory education in the nineteenth and early twentieth centuries, what may be termed token gestures to science education were contained in the curriculum. As the decades passed those gestures became more than token. Science became coequal, at least on the level of rhetoric, to other major features of the curriculum. Increasing the role of science in the curriculum of the public schools did not rest on a conception of young children as nascent scientists, as possessors of ways of thinking characteristically scientific, but rather on a stance of noblesse oblige—a kind of bringing of culture to the primitives, who on their own would have no interest in science. The task was to pour science into them, not to get science out of them. They were young children, not young scientists. They were unformed and unforming creatures; they needed to be formed, and when they were formed they would understand science and scientists. They were expected to understand science, not to *do* it except by repeating what great minds had done. To the students, science meant copying, duplicating what someone else had done. (They were "taught" science the way they were taught art.) In practice science was an exercise in memorization.

The third reason is that in the post–World War II era science education in the United States came to be judged as an almost total disaster. The conclusion was that schoolchildren did not understand science; that they were uninterested in, actively disliked, or actively sought to avoid exposure to science education; and that our status in the world as a nation was imperiled by the relative paucity of students who sought careers in science. Students were seen as victims of a stultifying, interest-extinguishing, outmoded science curriculum. In short, science education was a national disgrace, a waste of talent, and a threat to our preeminence in the world. This state of affairs was seen primarily in utilitarian terms (that is, in terms of the national interest) and only secondarily in terms of a more productive development of individual capabilities. This emphasis was starkly illuminated when the Russians orbited the first Sputnik in 1957 and we became Avis to their Hertz. We experienced that event as a potentially lethal threat to our place in the world. The reaction was dramatically swift. The science curriculum in our schools needed a complete overhaul. And so we got the "new" math, the "new" biology, the "new" physics (and even the "new" social studies). More than thirty years later, nothing has changed, and some are arguing that the situation is worse than ever. Every criticism made about the old curriculum is being made of the new ones. Indeed, as I write these words, the national media tell us of new reports by prestigious groups indicting science education in our schools.[1]

It is, I trust, obvious why I bring science education into a discussion of artistic activity. Why did such a well-intentioned effort to stimulate, influence, and enlarge the capabilities of students in a particular direction fail? Why did the assumption that students were capable of understanding and doing science *at a level appropriate to their cognitive development* not get confirmed? For my purposes it is crucial to emphasize that this assumption reflects a body of psychological research that made a shambles of the belief that the minds of children, even very young children, did not contain in some nascent form all the precursors, the seeds, so to speak, of scientific thinking. (This, of course, is precisely

1. To explain why science education is as counterproductive today as in earlier decades, why public education generally will not improve, is a complicated story I cannot go into here. I have written three books on these issues: *The Preparation of Teachers: An Unstudied Problem in Education, The Culture of the School and the Problem of Change* and *Schooling in America: Scapegoat and Salvation.*

what I have said about artistic activity.) As I said in an earlier chapter, Piaget gained recognition in the post–World War II era because his writings were so revelatory of how from the earliest days the child's cognitive capabilities unfolded and developed in stages to the point where the child could think objectively. Just as to Schaefer-Simmern the scribbles of children were not just scribbles, and just as to Koch the earliest efforts of his students to put imagery into words were not gibberish, so to Piaget the earliest efforts of children to comprehend their world, to assimilate and to accommodate to it, were not random affairs but the earliest manifestations of cognitive development that required nurturing. To be insensitive to the significance of these manifestations—worse yet, to ignore them—was to miss the opportunity to strengthen a developing capability. Unfortunately, that is precisely the opportunity the curriculum reformers missed totally. As I indicated in chapter 4, Piaget took a dim view, to say the least, of the misapplications of his work to education.

If in regard to artistic activity we are not to make all the mistakes of the science-curriculum reformers, several points need to be kept in mind. I am tempted to say that the first point is a glimpse of the obvious, at least among developmental psychologists. But if it is obvious in those circles, part of their worldview of children, it has not been assimilated by others in ways that lead to appropriate actions. I refer to the fact that curiosity is a distinguishing feature of young children. We can stimulate curiosity in them about this or that, but the fact is that independent of whatever we do, the child is a curious, question-asking organism, even before it has acquired language. The importance of this intrinsic curiosity cannot be overestimated because it is such a powerful goad to thinking and action and provides us with clues to what is interesting to the child. To the extent that we ignore or are insensitive to these clues, or seek to direct them in ways we think are important, we run the risk of diluting the strength of curiosity.

The task, and it is a difficult one, is how to capitalize on that curiosity so that the child's interests and sense of efficacy are broadened and strengthened. It is a matter of starting where the child is and then guiding and stimulating the child in ways consistent with expressed interests and level of cognitive development. We are, or should be, walking a fine line between where the child is and where we want him or her to go. Permissiveness and indulgence should not be confused with guidance, just as stimulation according to predetermined criteria or arbitrary schedules should not be confused with educating the child, if by educating we mean "leading out" what is in the mind of the child.

The educational process is neither a mindless indulgence nor a mindless pouring in. Science education can never be accused of mindless indulgence, but its grotesque failures can be blamed on its emphasis on pouring in predigested information that is unpalatable or incomprehensible to the child. That the child looks at the world with awe and wonder, that the child is constantly asking him- or herself questions about self and the world—why the sky is blue, why and how airplanes stay in the sky, why we see pictures on television or hear voices from a radio—seems to have totally escaped the curriculum developers. What requires explanation is why science education has not extinguished interest and curiosity in *every* student. Fairness requires me to note that this subversion begins for most children before they come to school. Science education in the schools very effectively and formally finishes the job of extinguishing awe and wonder about the world.

The preschool child is not viewed as a budding scientist—a question-asker, a manipulator, an experimenter, a "natural" when it comes to "the more you know the more you need to know." The works of Piaget and others have had no educational impact. Similarly, the child is not viewed as an artist despite the overwhelming evidence of artistic activity in all children in all cultures. One could argue that art education has the questionable good fortune (unlike science education) of being an insignificant part of formal schooling. If art education ever is given a more significant role in formal schooling, one has to hope that the lessons to be learned from the failures of science education will be drawn. If the reader has concluded that I am a passionate advocate for recognizing the importance of artistic activity not only for personal and cognitive development but also for providing opportunities over a lifetime for artistic expression, that reader is absolutely right. But if that same reader concludes that I am calling for more art education in our schools, that reader will be wrong.

Relevant here is a recent essay by Governor Thomas Kean of New Jersey titled "The 'Imperative' of Arts Education" (*Education Week*, March 1, 1989, p. 36). I think the reader will agree that we are not used to reading an article by a political figure, a policy-making person, that articulates so well the significance of artistic activity for individuals and the culture. I reprint it in its entirety because the essay implicitly contains a diagnosis that undercuts its major recommendation for a program in the arts.

> While a back-to-basics movement has figured prominently in the reform agenda of recent years, one "basic" has not been taken along for the ride on the bandwagon: arts education.

Our children can only suffer from schools' inattention to the performing arts, literature, visual art, and design. Sound training in these areas can not merely enrich their educational experience but also help prepare them for careers in the economy of the future.

In New Jersey, we are re-evaluating arts education and working to find ways to better incorporate it into the school curriculum. To this end, the state legislature has created a 22-member Literacy in the Arts Task Force.

A report released last spring by the National Endowment for the Arts— "Toward Civilization"—reached the unsettling conclusion that "basic arts education does not exist in the United States today."

The arts have often been dismissed as but another educational frill, little more than an entertaining diversion from ordinary classroom fare and perhaps even a contributing factor in the decline of public education.

To many ears, "arts education" harks back to the permissive educational environs of the last few decades. It sounds a bit too "touchy-feely"—too dependent on ill-defined criteria of personal response—to fit comfortably in the stern vocabulary of current education reforms.

No doubt the skepticism of many Americans towards arts education is born of personal experience. Too many of us can remember classes in which art meant learning a simple tune on the recorder or making a macrame potholder for our mothers. And we can all recall English classes in which studying literature meant reading the occasional novel or poem and certainly never included creative writing of our own. Though such experiences are more a symptom of the problem we face than a critique of arts education, they hold sway over parents and educators alike.

But Americans' distrust of arts education runs deeper than personal experience. As a people, we have always had a no-nonsense attitude towards education. The mission of the public schools in our democracy has been to provide young Americans with the basic tools for citizenship and employment.

While continuing to sing the praises of the three R's, we have gradually expanded this mission. Today, we expect our schools to teach technological literacy, prevent drug abuse, and even educate students about AIDS. But the potential of the arts to contribute to the basic goals of our public schools has always been discounted.

What, then, makes the arts so important? Why dedicate scarce time and money to their history, performance, and appreciation when children are struggling to learn to read and write, add and subtract?

Perhaps the foremost reason, in this competitive age, is that people who can communicate through the subtleties of the arts will have the skills and understanding that our 21st-century economy will require. The thespian will move from the stage to the boardroom with the self-confidence and range of intellect so vital to both. The engineer who has studied painting will grasp the "utility" of beauty in a world of increasingly sophisticated design. And the talented writer will stand astride our information age.

Creativity and expressiveness will be valuable commodities in an economy that places a premium on adaptability. As a recent report on "workplace basics" puts it, "Increasingly, skills such as problem-solving, listening, negotiation, and knowing how to learn are being seen as essentials." The "frill" of art may well provide the best career training a solicitous parent could hope for.

But the arts offer more than good job training. They have a unique capacity to capture and express human experience; what unites them is their power to convey truths about life that escape the probing eye of social and natural science.

Art makes us feel. It adds meaning to our lives by vividly evoking those qualities that our civilization holds dear: beauty, courage, justice, liberty, love of family and country. And it points out our failings when we fall short of these standards. The arts are part of the glue that binds one generation of Americans to the next, and the whole American experiment to the enterprise of Western civilization.

Our moral and ethical traditions are exemplified in our art. Dozens of courses explicitly dedicated to ethics cannot approach "Macbeth" for conveying the nature of ruthless self-promotion, cannot approximate Rupert Brooke's poetry for capturing the grim reality of war, and cannot match Norman Rockwell's prints for teaching the simple lessons of American life.

Art allows us to ask those questions that have forever occupied humankind. We can ponder our ultimate destiny on the back of Melville's Moby Dick, in the intent gaze of Rodin's "Thinker," or on the weary feet of Dante's pilgrim in "The Divine Comedy." As George Bernard Shaw wrote, "You use a glass mirror to see your face; you use works of art to see your soul."

By nurturing the creative impulse in our schools, we can ensure that our artistic tradition will continue. And in doing so, we will give our children skills and sensitivities that are simply not to be found in diagramming a sentence, doing long division, or dissecting a frog.

Art also serves as an ambassador of understanding, both within our diverse nation and among the nations of the world. If the plays of Arthur Miller give us a glimpse into American character, can we not learn about the Japanese from their Kabuki theater? If the colorful murals of the barrio can convey the rhythms of Hispanic life in the United States, should we not study the solemn visages of Russian Orthodox icons and the cold, mechanistic aesthetic of Soviet propaganda posters to know the Russians better?

New Jersey's task force—composed of educators, artists, and administrators—will outline a model arts curriculum for kindergarten through 12th grade and seek ways to provide the money and teachers that expanded arts education will require.

We have a long way to go—in New Jersey as in the rest of the country. But our goal is worthy of the other educational reforms we have seen in the last several years.

Artistic literacy is no less an imperative than general literacy. As Ernest L. Boyer, president of the Carnegie Foundation for the Advancement of Teaching and chairman of the New Jersey Literacy in the Arts Task Force, has so aptly put it: "Now, more than ever, all people need to see clearly, hear acutely, and feel sensitively through the arts. These skills are no longer just desirable. They are essential if we are to survive together with civility and joy."

We all must share Mr. Boyer's sense of urgency. The appeal of the arts is universal, their purpose is clear, and they deserve a place in our schools.

Several things are remarkable in this essay. For one thing, the essay would make no sense if it simply assumed that all children are capable in some way at some level of engaging in and deriving satisfaction from artistic activity. That assumption is not unusual or infrequent, except that it is honored far more in the breach than in practice. What is distinctive in the essay is that Governor Kean seeks to provide opportunities for development across the spectrum of the arts. He is talking about much more than what is conventionally called the visual arts. Far from regarding it as a "frill" or a token gesture to "culture," or only as a pleasurable hobby or recreation, he regards artistic activity as a way of understanding self, others, and other cultures. Artistic activity is an *imperative* for productive living for everyone. In saying so, the governor sets himself apart from most other people in the public, professional, and educational arenas.

Explicit in the governor's essay is a diagnosis: what passes for arts education in our schools is taught in ways that are anti-artistic and that rob the activity of its intended purposes. Implicit in this diagnosis is a more sweeping diagnosis: what is true for arts education is no less the case for the teaching of other subject matter—including science education. When the governor says, "Too many of us can remember classes in which art meant learning a simple tune on the recorder or making a macrame potholder for our mothers. And we can recall English classes in which studying literature meant reading the occasional novel or poem and certainly never included creative writing of our own," he is describing a general state of affairs, not one peculiar to arts education.

Given such a diagnosis, why should one expect that developing and implementing an arts curriculum for kindergarten through twelfth grade will be less stultifying and self-defeating than it is now? Why should the new curriculum be more successful than the reforms of the science curriculum? The problem, of course, is not one of curriculum but rather of the conception of how to mine and direct the interests and capabilities of children—more correctly, of how we understand the naturally occurring artistic activities of children. The governor is surely correct when he says, "Though such experiences are more a symptom of the problem than a critique of arts education, they hold sway over parents and educators alike." But why do they hold such sway?

At its root the answer is that artistic activity is regarded as a special feature of special people who alone can derive satisfaction from it over their lifetimes. It is understandable that parents and educators who hold this view and who regard themselves as devoid of creativity will ignore or be insensitive to artistic activity in children. But let us recognize that the task is not to devise a new curriculum but to confront the way we understand human nature, an understanding that is always suffused with a worldview derived from history and culture. The imperative in arts education is to take seriously what has been learned about the capabilities of children and about the context in which those capabilities are recognized and nurtured. If we know anything, it is that our schools do not make for sustained, productive, satisfying learning about self, others, and the world. Whatever has been wrong in arts education has been wrong in education generally. That is no less true at the university level, as Eisner (1989) has so pithily described.

To elaborate on these issues, and to underscore the complexity of factors we have to understand before we fly into action, I turn now to a book by David Feldman, a developmental psychologist. *Nature's Gambit* (1986) has received little attention, but I regard it as truly seminal. It is a book about six child prodigies: "a child who read music before he was four, two children who played winning chess before they entered school, another who studied abstract algebra in grade school, a youngster who produced typed scripts of original stories and plays before his fifth birthday, and a child who read, wrote, began learning foreign languages and composed short musical pieces before he was out of diapers" (p. 3) The book is distinctive both as description and as an effort at comprehensive explanation. I shall briefly summarize those parts of this theorizing that are most relevant to my purposes, but the summary inevitably will be no substitute for the richness and incisiveness of Professor Feldman's effort.

1. "If we can understand better how and why the prodigy does what he does, we will have made some substantial progress toward understanding how talent can be developed in general. For while the

prodigy's talent and progress are indeed out of the usual course of nature, the processes that control his development are not. In short the prodigy exhibits the very same kinds of developmental processes that the rest of us do, but because their abilities are so extraordinary it is especially revealing to observe these processes at work" (p. 9).

It is worthy of emphasis that Professor Feldman does not regard prodigies as a kind of sport in nature, the significance of which has little or no bearing on the development of talent in people generally. Prodigies are special, but their specialness illuminates the interplay of factors at work in all human development.

2. "While prodigies may or may not be talented in the sense of more generalized intellectual prowess, they do not demonstrate extraordinary performance across the board. Instead they seem extremely well matched to a particular environment, pretuned to grasp and master one particular area of endeavor. The prodigy is the most precociously specialized specialist that we know about. Indeed, the calling card of the prodigy is a tenacious commitment to do one specific thing at all costs: to see doing that thing as absolutely essential for satisfaction, expression, and well-being" (p. 10).

3. "'Co-incidence' is the general process of development that is revealed through study of the prodigy. The exploration of this process is the major organizing theme for this book. I have used the term 'co-incidence' to capture the melding of the many sets of forces that interact in the development and expression of human potential. With prodigies the co-inciding of forces tends to be more sharply defined and their interactions more dramatic than in the development of potential in the average individual. It is therefore easier with the prodigy to see what these forces are and how they influence the child's developing mastery. However, the forces and processes of co-incidence operate in the same general way for prodigy and non-prodigy alike. Thus, understanding something of the dynamic underlying the process of prodigious development will yield information about the general development of ability. It is the fortuitous convergence of highly specific individual proclivities with specific environmental receptivity that allows a prodigy to emerge. This is an infrequent and unlikely event. The convergence is not simply between two unitary, looming giants—an individual and an environment—but between a number of elements in a very delicate interplay: it includes a cultural milieu; the presence of a particular domain which is itself at a particular level of development; the avail-

ability of master teachers; family recognition of extreme talent and commitment to support it; large doses of encouragement and understanding; and other features as well" (pp. 11–12).

4. "It is critical to keep in mind that a prodigy is first and foremost a person living during a certain era, within a particular family, and with a wealth of other, nonprodigious life experiences. It is important to comprehend what the individual life course of a prodigy is like, how it is similar to and different from the life experiences of the rest of us, and how the individuals fit into the eras in which they live and work" (p. 12).

5. "The prodigy-to-be must encounter and master a specific body of knowledge and skill with which prodigious abilities will be expressed. The potential to perform at a high level in a particular field may not be activated or developed if the field, which is itself structured and developing along a certain pathway, is not available in a way that is comprehensible to the young mind. Bodies of knowledge are themselves cumulative, distilled products of many individuals' efforts to master and extend a field. Fields change in both their substantive base and the forms in which the knowledge is codified" (pp. 12–13).

6. "Cultures vary in the importance they attach to the mastery of different domains at different times. At a particular time and place pursing a specific field may be rewarded, ignored, or even punished. In the United States today serious chess players find that the lack of institutional interest or support often undermines their efforts to sustain a commitment to the game. In contrast, the Soviet Union has developed a well-organized system for detecting, developing, and supporting chess talent. The reverse is true for entrepreneurial activities in the two countries. Thus it is not enough to know that a child has great talent for a specific field, nor is it enough to know that a field is developed to a point where it is possible to engage an develop a given child's potential. Child and domain must be brought together under circumstances advantageous for sustained engagement. It may also be that certain kinds of prodigies will only appear and develop when a culture is itself organized to recognize and nurture excellence in that particular domain" (pp. 13–14).

Prodigies are indeed rare, but, as Professor Feldman stresses, that is because the coincidence of the interplay of certain factors is rare. For my purposes two of these factors are of special importance. The first is what he has appropriately termed receptivity, not only by the culture generally but by the immediate, concrete social-familial context.[2] If that context is unreceptive, whatever the reason, the child's display of interest or talent subsides or even disappears. In the six cases Feldman studied, that context was receptive in the most sensitive ways. Some might ask: how could the parents of these six prodigies *not* be receptive to the display of their children? But that is the point: *these* parents were receptive, but it does not follow that all parents would recognize, be receptive to, and nurture the display. It follows from Professor Feldman's position that if prodigies are rare it is because the coincidence of factors is rare. Prodigies are not explainable by an individual psychology that rivets on the discrete organism but by a rare, delicate interplay of factors including but not limited to individual psychology. Receptivity is more than awareness or sensitivity; it is powered by a value judgment that requires nurturing and stimulating reactions to what is displayed. If I emphasize receptivity, it is because that is what is absent in regard to artistic activity. A lack of receptivity not only reflects insensitivity to the presence of artistic activity, a lack of understanding of its cognitive and personal significance, but also a kind of cultural devaluation of that activity. In his efforts to understand prodigies, Professor Feldman presents us with a perspective that illuminates much more than the prodigy phenomenon. That is precisely what he set out to do, and he has done it creatively and well.

> The prodigy cannot answer all our questions about how development works or tell us what human history is about. Yet the phenomenon can draw our attention to aspects of human experience that, when understood more fully, may help illuminate both development and history. Development is a process that requires an understanding of the influence of several broad time frames as well as the coordination of individual qualities of mind and temperament with domains of knowledge that have their own histories, customs, pedagogies, and values. Understanding and learning to harness the factors influ-

2. The reader should consult a paper by Feldman and Goldsmith (1986) titled "Transgenerational Influences on the Development of Early Prodigious Behavior: A Case Study Approach." The case is that of the violinist Yehudi Menuhin, one of the most celebrated prodigies of this century. It is a fascinating account, really two independent accounts, of him and his family, justifiably permitting Feldman and Goldsmith to conclude: "If early experience is to be understood, and particularly if early influences on the development of talent are to be understood, then transgenerational influences will have to be taken seriously. The study of musical ability and achievement in extreme cases like Yehudi Mehuhin seems to be a promising place to begin" (p. 83).

encing development should make it possible to better facilitate matches between individuals and domains. Such efforts at optimizing individual expression of ability will, in turn, enrich existing domains or lead to the construction of new ones, thus raising the probability that more people will find the path to express their unique potential. Clearly this view of development, inspired by the experience of observing prodigies, is one that encompasses much more than simple survival. It assumes that each person has something unique to say and desires to use his or her unique mix of talents and experiences to leave a lasting mark. Development means satisfaction and fulfillment, not just survival, and somehow in that desire for fulfillment humanity strives to give meaning to its own history. Through that process new possibilities for expression are created, and the long-term well-being of the species is enhanced. (P. 231).

There is a facet to receptivity that Professor Feldman does not gloss over, and it has to do with teachers and teaching. I emphasize it here because of the justification it provides for what I consider distinctive in Schaefer-Simmern and Kenneth Koch as teachers. I have argued, as Professor Feldman does, that the conceptual task of the teacher in regard to any subject matter or activity is to have a clear picture of how it arises, unfolds, and gets transformed as the child develops. It would be more correct to say that the teacher must know not only how a subject-matter domain has come to be structured (that is, its organizing principles, its part-whole relationships, its generative purposes, its hierarchical properties)—what we mean or should mean when we say a teacher should "know" the subject matter—but, no less crucially, how that subject matter arises in or can be related to a child's experience. *The subject matter is already in some form, at some level, in the child's experience.* It is unlabeled, unorganized, but the ingredients are there. To Koch or Schaefer-Simmern, their students were poets and artists before they met them. Their task was to capitalize on that fact, not to approach the students as if they were empty vessels into which one poured knowledge or animals in a maze which had to be taught how to traverse it without "error." They were respectful of and receptive to beginnings indigenous to the child's interests and experience. They were stimulators, guiders, opportunity makers.

It is easy to say that one begins where the child is. This has the ring of truth, as do all clichés. But the problem with a cliché is that it does not tell you when and if your actions are consistent with that truth. It is easy to nod assent to the statement that one begins where the child is. What does that mean for how you guide a child so as to enable him or her to persist in that activity and to recognize and overcome problems peculiar to growth in that activity? Where the child is is one thing; where you want him or her to go is another thing. How to integrate the two without doing violence to the child's intentions is the always difficult pedagogical task. Put in another way, how do you maintain that delicate balance between where the child is going and where you think *that* child should go if he or she is to experience a sense of self-initiated growth?

Let me illustrate the point by an example familiar to all readers. It concerns my daughter. When she was three or four years of age, she pointed to the interstices between the fingers of her hand and asked: "Daddy, why don't we have fingers here?" I chuckled. I am ashamed to say that the psychologist in me saw no special personal significance in the question—that is significance for where Julie was at that moment psychologically. So in a blithely unreflective manner, I replied: "That is the way people are made." My answer was, of course, a textbook example of insensitivity to "where the child is." My comeuppance was immediate: "So, tell me, Daddy, how *are* people made?" I was then faced with the pedagogical task: how do I provide her with information that is appropriate to "where she is," that will give her food for thought, that will set the stage for and facilitate asking in the near future other predictable questions about the domain of sexual activity? In Professor Feldman's terms, sexual activity is a domain of knowledge that has structure and organization. It is not a random collection of facts. I knew a good deal about that domain. Julie was struggling with questions about that domain. How could I support that struggle, so central to her interests, so that the struggle remained productive, a source of continuing curiosity to her, not a struggle that went underground and became unproductive, an obstacle to a sense of accomplishment and satisfaction?

To be receptive to a child's artistic activity requires more than receptivity in the narrow sense. It requires understanding of the artistic process; of the intentions of the child as reflected in the relationships among the formal properties of the product (its gestalt properties); sensitivity to whatever difficulties the child has encountered and predictably will encounter as the activity proceeds over time; and the knack of making suggestions that are not prescriptive but may allow the child to perceive difficulties and opportunities in alternative ways. Being receptive means having a clear and integrated understanding of two domains: the artistic process and the world and capabilities of children.

That is a receptivity that Koch and Schaefer-Simmern had. Schaefer-Simmern had long been an artist in his own right, and that is no less true of Koch. They had experienced the struggles and satisfactions inherent in any artistic activity, how truly developmental a process it is: how one makes and is made, and how both processes are prologue to another phase in which one makes and is made. They respected their own unfolding too much to be disrespectful of "where a student is." They understood the world and the capabilities of children.

Some may argue that both men are "great" teachers, so exceptionally knowledgeable and talented that it is foolhardy to expect that more than a few other people could learn to do what they did. Is it not courting disillusionment to develop an arts education curriculum for our schools expecting that it will be taught by the likes of these two "greats"? It is, again, one of those "a few have it, most do not have it" arguments. Of course these two men are great teachers, but it does not follow that others lack the capacity to think the way they think and do what they did, albeit with less sophistication and dramatic accomplishments. To fall short of the ideal is no disgrace. What is both inexcusable and wasteful is to conclude or be taught that because you cannot scale the heights you had better choose other goals or, worse yet, simply stop climbing.

Throughout this book I have argued against the belief that artistic activity is a special feature of special people. I am here arguing against a view that says that there are very few teachers like Koch and Schaefer-Simmern and that the bulk of teachers lack what they have. This view misses the point: those who self-select themselves to become teachers are capable of approximating *at some level* an integration of knowledge of the artistic process, an understanding of children, and actions appropriate to that knowledge and understanding. To expect less of teachers is to get less from them and to confirm again the force of the self-fulfilling prophecy.

What the reader should ask is why what Schaefer-Simmern and Koch stand for is so rare in our schools. Not absent, but so rare as to cause a perceptive person like Governor Kean to indict arts education. And when that question is pursued the reader will begin to understand that what these men stand for will require a radical change in our conventional picture of schools. It is not a matter of changing a curriculum but of changing a view of what children are and of the conditions that make for productive learning. And it is not a matter of arts education alone, because whatever is wrong with arts education is no less true for other subject matter in our schools. If you accept the indictment of arts education, the dominoes of which the schools are built begin to fall.

But let us not scapegoat teachers and schools. They are victims of a worldview that rests on axioms invalid in whole or in part. Schools will change in desirable ways only when those within education who stand for what Schaefer-Simmern and Koch stand for (what Dewey and Piaget also stand for) receive support from those outside of schools. It is when pressure from without is consistent with pressure from within that change becomes possible. Today, the pressure from without represents a stance that is the polar opposite of what Koch, Schaefer-Simmern, Dewey, and Piaget stand for. Governor Kean's diagnosis is correct. But the substance of this cure, a new curriculum, is part of the problem, not its solution. We know how to change curricula. We are inexpert in fathoming and uncovering the invalid axioms on which such changes are based. The history of arts education is the story of how the nature of human nature can at best be ignored and, at worst, destroyed.

II ◆ THE SOCIETAL SIGNIFICANCE OF ARTISTIC ACTIVITY

The significance of art can be viewed from many perspectives. Certainly one of the most frequently encountered concerns aesthetic response: why works of art elicit the reactions they do; why reactions change over days, years, and centuries; why some works of art gain celebrity and then lose their power to attract and satisfy. A related perspective is the historical one, which seeks to understand and account for continuities and discontinuities in the contents, organization, appearances, and social functions of works of art. Typical of this perspective is the study of individual artists in the present or near or distant past, in order to fathom the origins and development of their artistic styles and to place their works and lives in the society of their times. How do you account for their innovativeness, for their impact on other artists, for the rise and decline (if any) of their creativity, or for their changing status in the pantheon of artists?

Still another perspective, more recent than the others, is economic. For example, John M. Montias, a professor of economics at Yale, has studied mid-seventeenth-century Delft, more specifically the guild of St. Luke, which regulated the arts and art-related crafts of the city. His book *Art and Artisans in Delft* contains a summary of all archival documents relating to guild practices, the apprenticeship of members, their contacts with clients and dealers, and their social status. From these documents Professor Montias deduces that the cost of becoming an artist was a formidable barrier to the sons of ordinary people and that the world of Dutch art was less egalitarian than is commonly supposed.

Today we are used to seeing and hearing news items about the escalating sums paid for works of art. These news items have little to say about artistic activity or even artistic quality, but they illuminate the dynamics of fashion, conspicuous consumption, "acquiring culture," and the tendency for everything and everybody to be caught up in a market economy. (In February 1989, a subsidiary of Chase-Manhattan Bank began plans to raise $300 million from pension funds to invest in artwork.) Aside from the implications that can be drawn from regarding art in the same way as the listings on the New York Stock Exchange or wheat, pork bellies, or soy beans on the diverse commodity exchanges it should not go unnoticed that the label "art" refers to only one type of visual art, reinforcing the narrowest view of art and non-art.

These different perspectives have one theme in common: artists and their works are not comprehensible apart from era, culture, and an undergirding worldview. That does not mean, of course, that at any one time and place there were no differences among artists in style, content, composition, and other formal characteristics. But those differences, artistic and personal-idiosyncratic, did not have socially virginal origins. They arose from contexts and in turn influenced those contexts. Today it is hard to avoid the impression that each week a new approach to art is proclaimed that distinguishes itself from all other approaches, past and present, and that seeks to become the new tradition. The labels multiply, the number of art galleries seems to increase exponentially, and competition for recognition in the news media is fierce indeed, bordering sometimes on the nasty. The optimist will regard this state of affairs as an explosion of creativity. The cynic will regard it as a reflection of an unbridled destructive need to be different, to be shocking, to develop one's own signature. Neither cynic nor optimist would deny that this state of affairs is incomprehensible apart from what has happened in Western society in the past century, and some would go back much further in time.

We have learned a great deal about art and society from these different perspectives. But they are not helpful in regard to the approach I have adopted in this book. My perspective derives from an assumption for which the evidence is scanty but compelling: the capacity to engage in artistic activity is inherent in all human beings. Once you make that assumption, you then confront the identical theme and conclusion that all the other perspectives have in common. How do we account for the *presence,* recognition, and development of artistic activity? How do we account for the *absence* of such activity in most people? Both questions imply an answer that involves, among other things, social-cultural features and their relation to an underlying worldview. As I indicated earlier, the perspective I have adopted and the questions to which it gives rise are in all respects similar to those articulated in regard to the capabilities of women and blacks. Those who in the past served as advocates for these groups had no difficulty pointing to individuals in these groups who had accomplished much. Those who opposed their advocacy did not question those instances of indubitable accomplishments. They regarded these individuals as exceptions, as special in ways that did not justify generalizing to the larger group, that did not invalidate conclusions about incapacity of the group of which they were a member. For the advocates, these "exceptions" had enormous significance for understanding the absence of accomplishment in these groups. The controversy is by no means over, but whatever evidence we have, if it does not "prove" the advocate's position, lends more than a little comfort to it.

The perspective I have adopted in regard to artistic activity will arouse no controversy, if by controversy you mean the struggle, passion, and militancy that have marked exchanges between partisans for and against changing views about the capabilities of women and blacks. Even those who find themselves agreeing with my perspective will feel no call to the barricades. And, of course, those who disagree will make short shrift of my argument and go on to "truly" important issues. The idea that artistic activity is universal sounds virtuous or utopian, but like many virtues it is unexciting. As someone said to me: "We have gotten along for centuries without taking your perspective seriously. Why should you expect that *now* it should receive a hearing?" Let me answer this question with another question: What brought about a change in this country in our attitude toward slavery? The answer, of course, is complex, requiring discussion of religious, political, constitutional, economic, and moral considerations. For purposes of simplification, one can begin by saying that slaves were denied the opportunity to be other than what they were. There were many abolitionists who judged the capabilities of blacks to be inherently inferior to those of whites, but their advocacy derived from the belief that blacks could be more than they were, that they deserved the right to productively use and develop their limited potentials. To deny them the opportunity to use their capabilities was sinful, a form of human abuse. The abolitionists and their opponents alike agreed that there were blacks whose capabilities and accomplishments matched those of whites, but they were seen as "exceptions," not prodromal of what all other blacks might do or become if slavery were abolished. Nevertheless, that was no excuse for denying blacks the opportunity to develop whatever capabilities they had.

As I read the literature on slavery, another factor, psychological in the narrow sense, made it extraordinarily difficult for many people to tolerate slavery: their capacity to identify with the plight of slaves. It is as if they said: "How would I feel if I were prevented from developing any sense of personal mastery or expression, the sense that you have put your personal stamp on some activity or product reflective of what you think and are. How does it feel to go through life never to experience at any level in any way the experience of creative agency?" These questions reflect a process that allows us today to imagine what it is like to live in a country where you cannot say what you want to say, write what you want to write, travel where you want to travel, work where you want to work, worship in the way you want to worship, and read what you want to read. It is a process that illuminates aspects of our existence at the same time that it points to the darkness in the lives of others. It is a process that reminds us of what we have that others do not have.

But how can this process play a role if we do not see any difference between ourselves and others? Concretely, if most people regard themselves as lacking the ability to engage in artistic activity, and they are reinforced in countless ways in such a self-regard, they have no basis whatsoever for understanding its negative consequences. It is hard to get upset about a lack in others when that lack is a characteristic of you, especially if in other respects you see similarities with those others. Blacks and women have long had their articulate, militant advocates. But for all practical purposes there are no advocates for artistic activity as a crucial factor in living, the absence of which consigns people to an impoverished existence. There *are* advocates for the arts, but mostly they seek funding to support the activities and settings of that very small group who meet the conventional criteria of who is and who is not an artist. Indeed, most of these advocates subscribe to the view that artistic activity is a special feature of special people, so special to the culture as to deserve special recognition and support. Their advocacy is justified on two grounds: it preserves and supports the works of artists, past and present, who have contributed to our cultural heritage (what some have termed "high culture"), and it makes these works available for appreciation by the general public.

None of these perspectives or the programs to which they have given rise has addressed this question: what are the consequences for individuals when they go through life never experiencing the sense of mastery and satisfaction from engaging in an artistic activity? What happens to people who regard themselves as devoid of the capability of doing or making something that bears their distinctive imprint? The post–World War II era has been characterized as one in which equality of opportunity has become a central societal value and concern. That concern did not arise out of the blue, or as a simple reflection of an elevated morality, or as a result of a heightened sensitivity to a democratic ethos. One of the dictionary definitions of concern is "an uneasy state of blended interest, uncertainty, and apprehension," and that well describes the growing unease people felt as they perceived and tried to understand changes taking place in the society. It is not hyperbole to say that for many people, young and old, the society was becoming unhinged as convention and custom were subjected to diverse challenge, especially by groups heretofore denied equality of opportunity. But these groups were only part of the story. The phrase *intergenerational conflict* became popular, except among those who thought that war was a more appropriate word than conflict.

It is risky, I know, to explain a complex picture and its history by a single factor, especially if that factor seems narrowly psychological. If I run that risk now it is for purposes of emphasis and because of the implications of that factor for artistic activity—that is, for the perspective I have adopted in this book. It goes like this: it is as if, with increasing strength in increasing numbers of people, growing up and becoming a part of the society began to be seen as a process that obliterated individuality, restricted modes of expressiveness, valued conformity more than creativity, was insensitive to the emptiness of the acquisitive life, and rendered personal authenticity impossible. These are more than psychological attitudes in the narrow sense. They are outcroppings of a changing worldview about the purposes of living, about the past and the future, about the nature of human nature. Granted that this changing worldview has origins in the distant as well as the near past, and granted that it is far from a coherent view in the sense of resting on axioms so generally accepted as not to require articulation, few people would deny either that tradition has lost its firm hold or that what they perceive as taking its place is cause for optimism.

There are, of course, a few people who find comfort in the position that we always misjudge the pace and significance of social change, that we confuse appearances with the underlying realities, that what *was* is valued more positively than what *is*, that we fear change and therefore devalue it, that we misinterpret turmoil as a harbinger of personal and societal decline. This is a position not without historical support, its proponents taking delight in pointing out how over the centuries many prophets of gloom and doom have been egregiously wrong. That the examples they quote are inevitably selective, that their position has a Panglossian flavor, that they literally cannot explain why in human history dramatic changes in worldviews have occurred some of which by no stretch of the imagination represented "progress"—these objections pose no problems for those who see man on an onward and upward climb to a peak of semiperfection.

I am not a prophet of doom. But I am also not one who views the current scene with optimism because the changes that are occurring have sharpened the antagonisms between two factors. The first factor is the articulated unwillingness of people to live lives that prevent or inhibit the sense of individuality, the sense that what one does is expressive of one's interests, abilities, and hopes. It is a matter of finding not only a place in this world but rather places in, through, and on which you put your individual mark. This is a desire as well as an expectation. As never before in human history, people—young and old, rich and poor, men and women—can see the world and the different opportunities it contains for individual fulfillment. And especially in the post–World War II era, what they see they have been encouraged to strive for and to expect. What is new in this picture is the strength of the conviction that there is far more to living than making a living. And the more is the opportunity to experience the feeling of worthiness deriving from the perception that one's capacities are productively utilized and that outlets for one's interests are available. The logo of my travel agent is: see the world before you leave it. In a changing worldview the phenomenological logo has become: experience the world before you leave it. Most people do not know it, of course, but they are using a concept of experience identical to that of John Dewey: a time-bounded interval during which the individual's capacities, interests, and energies have been integrated and engaged in ways that enliven and enlarge one's sense of self and purpose.

The second factor that contributes to an antagonism to the first factor can be put succinctly: in our society most people rarely experience the sense of individuality or individual fulfillment. This does not mean that they are clinical cases of depression and anxiety unable to derive any satisfaction from relationships, activities, and work (although the number of people who describe themselves as depressed and anxious has increased dramatically). What it does mean is that many people live with the sense that they have not had, do not have, or will not have the opportunity to test and express their capabilities, to feel distinctive in some way, to experience the sense of growth, to be uniquely creative in some respect. When we read about Schaefer-Simmern's mentally retarded and "ordinary" people or Kenneth Koch's ghetto schoolchildren and his uneducated, sick, passive, socially isolated, aged people in a nursing home, we have no difficulty comprehending the emptiness of their lives, the meaning of lack of opportunity, and the galvanizing response to opportunity to engage in a creative activity. Of course these individuals are in obvious ways an atypical sample of the general population. But they are not atypical in terms of regarding themselves as devoid of the capacity to give ordered expression to internal imagery in ways that not only give them pleasure but propel them to continue in the activity because of its promise of the sense of growth. The antagonism I am describing cuts across social-class lines. It is no less sharp, destabilizing, and destructive among the educated than among the underprivileged, a point very incisively discussed by Paul Wachtel in his book *The Poverty of Affluence* (1983).

By formal training and experience I, like Wachtel, am a clinical psychologist. I have supervised scores of clinical psychologists and I have interacted professionally with hundreds of them. And I have read the psychotherapy literature. It is no secret that most clients seen by psychotherapists are educationally and socioeconomically privileged. It is obvious that those who seek psychotherapy are at war with themselves, with others, or both. However varied they and their problems appear, they have in common a negative self-regard; in some respect they feel inadequate and unworthy. However, in the past decade I have become aware of a new complaint in people of all ages: the feeling that their expectations from life will have to be scaled down, that they will never be able to achieve what they had hoped, that their future is bleak. As one young woman who had a managerial position in a relatively large firm said: "I always expected that I would be going from one challenge to another, from one level of responsibility to another, that I had realizable goals. What I am beginning to see is that the challenges aren't really there except now and then, and mostly then. I am doing what I thought I would be doing but I am not feeling what I thought I would be feeling. What I did not expect is how hemmed in, straitjacketed and slotted I feel. I can't live with the thought that my best years are behind me." Or as a middle-aged owner of a business said: "I knew from the beginning that the most I could expect from this business is money. Mine is not an interesting business. What I did expect is that I could make it possible for my three children to have interesting lives, not like me to use only a small part of their brains. But I have had to give up that expectation. They are struggling, they seem to have no direction in life, they seem resigned, as if there is no point to working your butt off. And every time I think about them and what the rest of my life is probably going to be, I can cry. It's hard, very hard, to live with a daily sense of disappointment." Neither of these individuals nor the many others I could present came to psychotherapy because of difficulty adjusting to lowered expectations, or because they experienced their work as stifling, smothering, disappointing. That was not what they complained about when they began psychotherapy, but that is precisely what emerged over time. The sense that they could no longer expect much from life, that they were impotent to change their situation, let alone change a complicated, vast, uncomprehending, incomprehensible, overpowering world. Generally speaking, psychotherapists do not know how to deal with such a complaint except to view it as a derivative of intrapsychic or interpersonal conflict. That is no less than a scandalous trivialization of reality and will increasingly be a crucial problem in living.

In one of my graduate seminars I routinely bring up for discussion Ken Kesey's novel *One Flew Over the Cuckoo's Nest*. The first item I bring up is how mental hospitals are organized and why. Seminar discussions often do not proceed in a linear fashion, and mine certainly do not. What emerged from that discussion, what I was truly unprepared for, was the fear of a majority of the students that they, like McMurphy, would conform, would *have* to conform, to a life devoid of individuality, of creative expression. In all subsequent years that fear has always been articulated by some students.

As a nation we are having difficulty adjusting to the fact that we can no longer do what we want to do in the way we want to do it. We are enmeshed in a world system that has discernibly decreased our freedom of action. Power is one thing, freedom to use it is quite another. That is precisely the substance of a conflict within people in our nation: the belief that the expression of one's capabilities is on a collision course with bigness, complexity, impersonality, and conformity. This is true for some people. Many more have never gotten to the point where they believe they have capabilities or, if they allow themselves such a belief, they are fearful of articulating it.

The point of all this is not that a lot of people have a lot of problems, or that they are unhappy. So what else is new? What is new is that creativity has become one of the important goals in living. That, of course, is *not* the way people formulate the goal for themselves. But when people say they fear losing their individuality, that they feel unfulfilled, that they are bored and feel empty, or that they have put their imprint on nothing; or when they complain about their fruitless search for challenge and novelty: or when they mourn a past of great expectations and resign themselves to an impoverished future; or when they demean their capabilities for fear that testing them will bring failure—call these expressions what you will, explain them as you will, they reflect a need to be effective in ways that challenge and exploit capabilities, sustain interest, and propel one eagerly to a future.

The reader may wonder what relation, if any, exists between this changing worldview and artistic activity. I have to remind the reader of the two major themes that have occupied us in previous chapters: artistic activity is a universal feature in human behavior, and in our society people succumb to the view that artistic activity is a special gift of special people. They come to see themselves as uncreative, incapable at any level of creativity to put their stamp on anything, to make something that is expressive of their internal imagery, to feel psychological ownership because it is theirs and their alone. I also argued that the need, the yearning, the hunger to be artistic and creative never extinguishes. It goes underground, so to speak (unless a Schaefer-Simmern or a Kenneth Koch or someone like them miraculously leads it out). The negative consequences of this unfulfilled yearning depend on, among other things, the degree to which that yearning for individuality of expression encounters obstacles in other major areas of living. And therein is the special significance of artistic activity for today's changing worldview: the dysphoric consequences of the belief that one will be denied opportunities for individual expression, growth, and challenge—that one must scale down one's expectations and conform to mind-constricting "realities"—is precisely a belief that most people absorb early in life in regard to artistic activity. The difference, of course, is that in regard to artistic activity, it is a belief that they absorb *and* accept, whereas that same kind of belief in other areas of living involves conscious awareness and conflict. Most people regard themselves as having more capabilities than the future, the realities, will allow to be realized. They do not, of course, perceive their plight as in any way related to the ways in which they came to regard themselves as unartistic. And yet, the conflicts of which they are so conscious have at their core the need to put their imprint, their inner imagery, their sense of uniqueness on something somewhere in their lives.

You can explain, as many have, these perceptions and a changing worldview in terms of a complex history comprising political, economic, and religious factors. What tends to be underemphasized or ignored in these explanations are the implications of the strength that has been attached in the population generally to the need for the sense of individuality. At the same time that they have felt the need for community, the need to feel part of some supportive network of relationships, to feel the opposite of non-belongingness, they have felt a need to experience and demonstrate individuality. This is an old story in American history, described so well by de Tocqueville a century and a half ago.

It is not that people go around proclaiming their need for and lack of creative experience. To feel such a need is one thing, best left on the level of private thought and fantasy. To give voice to that need requires that to some degree at least you feel you can be creative, and that degree of positive self-regard is what is so frequently absent. What significances should be attached to the plethora of books, newspaper articles, and advertisements that contain the message that your hidden talents, your true self, can and should be developed and expressed? Why has the phrase "consciousness raising" become part of everyday parlance? Why has the phrase "alternative life styles" lost much of its pejorative status? What about the popularity of television and radio programs that encourage and instruct in "creative sex"? And then, of course, there is the phrase "realizing your potential," which is hard not to hear several times in the course of a day.

I do not regard these phrases and expressions as unalloyed blessings in the sense of being harbingers of a new and desirable level of personal expression and fulfillment. One can react to the current scene with satisfaction that the desire for individuality and creative expression seems to be as strong as it is in the general population. But one can also react with concern to the somewhat desperate, transient, superficial ways by which people seek to experience the sense of individuality and creative expression.

From the argument I have advanced in this book, the significance of artistic activity for comprehending the current scene is offered not as explanation but as an example of how conventional views of human abilities are indirectly and directly being challenged and transformed. It is more than an example because these are the same conventional views, the same psychology, that have made artistic activity off limits for most people. I would argue that the factors that engender attitudes of incapacity and impotence in artistic activity are the same factors that obstruct satisfaction in other activities. Nothing rivals artistic activity as a way of giving ordered and sustained expression to internal imagery and ideas. To *do* and *make* something in some medium that stands for *you*, something that is psychologically *yours*, something *you* have created and from which you derive satisfaction *despite* the judgments of comparative worth others may make of your efforts, a something that *makes you* just as you *make a thing*, is to experience the sense and pleasure of creativity. When such an activity is absent from one's life—which is to say that one has made nothing that bears one's personal imprint—and when that absence becomes correlated with lack of satisfaction in other arenas of living, the personal and social consequences can be a sustained source of frustration and emptiness. That is not to say that the absence of artistic activity in one's life inevitably dooms one to an impoverished existence. There are satisfactions that one can experience in other arenas of activity that are worthy and from which a sense of accomplishment can be derived. But, with most people, if that sense of accomplishment is absent or is fragile or turns out to be illusory, the disappointment and disillusionment receive added fuel from the fire of longstanding, culturally learned attitudes of uncreativeness. Artistic activity is no royal road to the good life. It is a way of using one's self, one's capacities. It is quintessentially an activity that one can perform and psychologically own. It is a way of learning about one's self and one's world. Both are changed in some way.

In a world in which few people feel needed or wanted, in which their presence or absence make no differences, the yearning for some way of impacting on that world has become, paradoxically, stronger, unfocused, inexorable, and destabilizing. The societal response has been predictably clinical: there are problems, and we must head off and dilute their destructive impacts. Our efforts at repair are political, economic, legal, and educational in conception and implementation. These efforts are as understandable as they are necessary. But they have all the limitations of the clinical model in that they are essentially reactive and not preventive. They are not preventive in the sense of recognizing that in contemporary Western societies the issue is only secondarily one of material being, of only "getting along," of improving equality of opportunity. What has become primary for people is that they can be more than they are. Put in another way, they expect more from life than in previous times, and that more in life is the sense of creativity. Phenomenologically speaking they do not, of course, pose the issue in terms of creativity. Indeed, the expectations are hardly formulated in a clear way. However differently they are felt and articulated—in hopes, language, and fantasy—they reflect the need to feel that they are using and expressing their interests and capabilities. It is not simply that they have high expectations. They are not like Schaefer-Simmern's or Koch's students, people without hope or expectation, consigned to a life of emptiness. They are not like people in underdeveloped countries for whom sheer survival is the primary goal in living. And they are not like people in totalitarian nations who resign themselves to a life of stultifying conformity. No, they are people who expect to experience accomplishment and, crucially, the sense of personal change and growth—that integration of capability, interest, challenge, and productive struggle so well illustrated by artistic activity. If they do not seek, have been taught not to seek, outlets in artistic activity, they nevertheless seek the equivalent.

I am not, of course, defending artistic activity, assigning it a vital role, because of its therapeutic implications or as a palliative for disappointments elsewhere in living. Indeed, I am not defending it in terms of conventional views of artistic activity because it is those views that contribute to people's self-image as incapable of engaging in artistic activity. What requires defense is the view that artistic activity is a universal human capability; inhibition and lack of recognition of this activity prevents us today from comprehending changes in worldview that pose problems for which our remedial efforts seem inadequate or self-defeating. Artistic activity is not on the societal agenda. It is not seen as a "social problem." It does not call for action. It is an activity that our psychologies regard as special in special people. And yet, these psychologies, by their focus on the individual psyche, distract us from examining how the early manifestations of artistic activity in all young people are aborted by the culture, thus robbing people of satisfaction from a unique feature of the human mind. We can no longer afford to regard the manifestations, development, and extinguishing of this feature only in terms of art; rather, we must see it as a symptom whose explanation will shed light on changes taking place in a world our society hardly understands.

REFERENCES

Asch, S. E. "Forming impressions of personality." *Journal of Abnormal and Social Psychology* 41 (1946): 258–90.

Baker, R. "Getting tired of high-culture humility." *New York Times*, Dec. 28, 1988.

Berta, R. "Henry Schaefer-Simmern's Legacy to Art Education: Unfolding His Figure and His Ground." Ph.D. diss., Stanford University School of Education, 1990.

Dewey, J. *Art as Experience*. New York: Minton and Balch, 1934.

———. "Interpretation of the savage mind." *Psychological Review* 1902: 217–30. Reprinted in J. Ratner, ed. *John Dewey: Philosophy, Psychology and Social Practice*. New York: Capricorn Books, 1965.

———. "Psychology as social practice." *Psychological Review* 1900: 105–24. Reprinted in Ratner, *John Dewey*.

———. "The reflex arc concept in psychology." *Psychological Review* 1896: 357–80. Reprinted in Ratner, *John Dewey*.

Dollard, J. *Criteria for the Life History*. New Haven: Yale University Press, 1935.

Eisner, E. W. *Cognition and Curriculum*. New York: Longman, 1982.

———. "Will the arts continue to occupy place at margins of educational institutions?" NAEA (National Art Education Association) *Advisory*, Fall 1989 (1916 Association Drive, Reston, Va., 22091).

Feldman, D. H. *Nature's Gambit*. New York: Basic Books, 1986.

Feldman, D. H., and L. T. Goldsmith. "Transgenerational influences on the development of early prodigious behavior: A case study approach." In W. Fowler, ed. *Early Experience and the Development of Competence*. San Francisco: Jossey-Bass, 1986.

Flexner, A. *Medical Education in the United States and Canada*. A report to the Carnegie Foundation for the Advancement of Teaching. Washington, D.C.: Carnegie Foundation for the Advancement of Teaching, 1960. Originally published in 1910.

Gardner, H. *The Arts and Human Development*. New York: John Wiley, 1973.

Hamilton, E. *The Ever-Present Past*. New York: W. W. Norton, 1964.

———. *Three Greek Plays*. New York: W. W. Norton, 1930.

Hampl, P. "The lax habits of the free imagination." *New York Times Book Review*, March 5, 1989.

Hilgard, E. *American Psychology in Historical Perspective: Addresses of Presidents of the American Psychological Association, 1892–1977*. Washington, D.C.: American Psychological Association, 1978.

James, W. *Talks to Teachers on Psychology.* London: Longmans, Green, 1899.

———. *The Varieties of Religious Experience*. 1902; Cambridge: Harvard University Press, 1985.

Kahler, E. *The Disintegration of Form in the Arts*. New York: Braziller, 1968.

Kamii, C., and R. De Vries. *Physical Knowledge in Preschool Education: Implications ·of Piaget's Theory.* Englewood Cliffs, N.J.: Prentice-Hall, 1978.

Kazan, E. *A Life*. New York: Knopf, 1988.

Kean, T. H. "The 'imperative' of arts education." *Education Week* 8, no. 23 (1989): 36.

Koch, K. *I Never Told Anybody.* New York: Random House, 1977.

———. *Wishes, Lies and Dreams*. New York: Chelsea House, 1970.

Lipman, S. "The NEA: Looking back, looking ahead." *New Criterion,* Sept. 1988: 6–7.

———. "Reflections on Bach." *New Criterion,* Sept. 1989: 50–53.

Montias, J. M. *Art and Artisans in Delft*. Princeton: Princeton University Press, 1982.

Ribe, N. M. "Atonal music and its limits." *Commentary* 84, no. 5: 49–54.

Richardson, E. *In the Early World*. New York: Pantheon, 1964.

Sarason, S. B. *The Culture of the School and the Problem of Change*. 2d ed. Boston: Allyn and Bacon, 1983.

———. *The Making of an American Psychologist: An Autobiography.* San Francisco: Jossey-Bass, 1988.

———. *Schooling in America: Scapegoat and Salvation*. New York: The Free Press, 1983.

———. *Work, Aging, and Social Change*. New York: The Free Press, 1977.

Schaefer-Simmern, H. W. *The Unfolding of Artistic Activity.* Berkeley: University of California Press, 1970.

———. Taped lectures nos. 11 and 13 given at St. Mary's College (Moraga, Calif.) in 1966.

Skinner, B. F. *Walden Two*. New York: Macmillan, 1976.

Spock, B. *Baby and Child Care*. New York: Pocket Books, 1945.

Stanislavski, C. *An Actor Prepares*. New York: Theater Arts Books, 1936.

Susskind, E. C. "Questioning and Curiosity in the Elementary School Classroom." Ph.D. dissertation, Yale University, 1969.

Wachtel, P. *The Poverty of Affluence*. New York: The Free Press, 1983.

Wertheimer, M. *Productive Thinking*. New York: Harper and Row, 1945.

Wolf, T. *Alfred Binet*. Chicago: University of Chicago Press, 1973.

INDEX

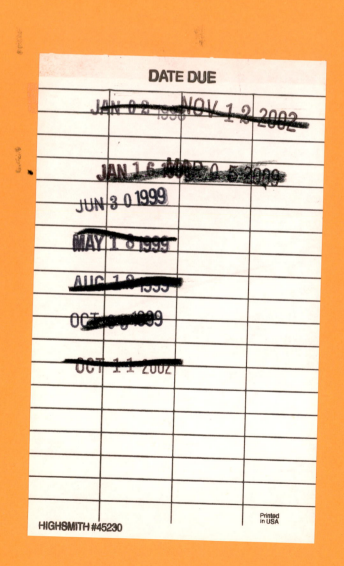

DATE DUE

JAN 0 2 1998 NOV 1 2 2002		
JAN 1 6 MAR 0 5 2000		
JUN 3 0 1999		
MAY 1 8 1999		
AUG 1 8 1999		
OCT 0 5 1999		
OCT 1 1 2002		

HIGHSMITH #45230

Printed
in USA